Main

LUCENT LIBRARY OF
BLACK HISTORY

HIDDEN

NO MORE African American Women in STEM Careers

By Caroline Kennon

Published in 2018 by
Lucent Press, an Imprint of Greenhaven Publishing, LLC
353 3rd Avenue
Suite 255
New York, NY 10010

Designer: Deanna Paternostro
Editor: Siyavush Saidian

Library of Congress Cataloging-in-Publication Data

Names: Kennon, Caroline, author.
Title: Hidden no more : African American women in STEM careers / Caroline
  Kennon.
Other titles: African American women in STEM careers
Description: New York : Lucent Press, c2018. | Series: Lucent library of
  Black history | Includes bibliographical references and index.
Identifiers: LCCN 2017041200 | ISBN 9781534562431 (library bound book) | ISBN 9781534562950
  (paperback book)
Subjects: LCSH: African American women scientists–Biography. | Women
  scientists–United States–Biography.
Classification: LCC Q130 .K46 2018 | DDC 509.2/52–dc23
LC record available at https://lccn.loc.gov/2017041200

Printed in the United States of America

CPSIA compliance information: Batch #CW18KL: For further information contact Greenhaven Publishing LLC, New York, New York at 1-844-317-7404.

Please visit our website, www.greenhavenpublishing.com. For a free color catalog of all our high-quality books, call toll free 1-844-317-7404 or fax 1-844-317-7405.

CONTENTS

FOREWORD

Black men and women in the United States have become successful in every field, but they have faced incredible challenges while striving for that success. They have overcome racial barriers, violent prejudice, and hostility on every side, all while continuing to advance technology, literature, the arts, and much more.

From medicine and law to sports and literature, African Americans have come to excel in every industry. However, the story of African Americans has often been one of prejudice and persecution. More than 300 years ago, Africans were taken in chains from their home and enslaved to work for the earliest American settlers. They suffered for more than two centuries under the brutal oppression of their owners, until the outbreak of the American Civil War in 1861. After the dust settled four years later and thousands of Americans—both black and white—had died in combat, slavery in the United States had been legally abolished. By the turn of the 20th century, with the help of the 13th, 14th, and 15th Amendments to the U.S. Constitution, African American men had finally won significant battles for the basic rights of citizenship. Then, with the passage of the groundbreaking Civil Rights Act of 1964, many people of all races began to believe that America was finally ready to start moving toward a more equal future.

These triumphs of human equality were achieved with help from brave social activists such as Frederick Douglass, Martin Luther King Jr., and Maya Angelou. They all experienced racial prejudice in their lifetimes and fought by writing, speaking, and peacefully acting against it. By exposing the suffering of the black community, they brought the United States together to try and remedy centuries' worth of wrongdoing. Today, it is important to learn about the history of African Americans and their experiences in modern America in order to work toward healing the divide that still exists in the United States. This series aims to give readers a deeper appreciation for and understanding of a part of the American story that is often left untold.

Even before the legal emancipation of slaves, black culture was thriving despite many attempts to suppress it. From the 1600s to the 1800s, slaves

4

developed their own cultural perspective. From music, to language, to art, slaves began cultivating an identity that was completely unique. Soon after these slaves were granted citizenship and were integrated into American society, African American culture burst into the mainstream. New generations of authors, scholars, painters, and singers were born, and they spread an appreciation for black culture across America and the entire world. Studying the contributions of these talented individuals fosters a sense of optimism. Despite the cruel treatment and racist attitudes they faced, these men and women never gave up, changing the world with their determination and unique voice. Discovering the triumphs and tragedies of the oppressed allows readers to gain a clearer picture of American history and American cultural identity.

Here to help young readers with this discovery, this series offers a glimpse into the lives and accomplishments of some of the most important and influential African Americans across historical time periods. Titles examine primary source documents and quotes from contemporary thinkers and observers to provide a full and nuanced learning experience for readers. With thoroughly researched text, unique sidebars, and a carefully selected bibliography for further research, this series is an invaluable resource for young scholars. Moreover, it does not shy away from reconciling the brutality of the past with a sense of hopefulness for the future. This series provides critical tools for understanding more about how black history is a vital part of American history.

SETTING THE SCENE:

1861
The American Civil War begins.

1865
The American Civil War ends, and slavery is abolished.

1861	1864	1865	1921	1934

1934
Ruth Howard becomes the first black woman to earn her PhD in psychology.

1864
Rebecca Lee Crumpler is the first African American woman to become a physician in the United States.

1921
Elizabeth Coleman becomes the first African American woman to earn a pilot's license.

A TIMELINE

1947
Marie Daly becomes the first black woman to earn her PhD in chemistry in the United States.

1960s
The African American civil rights movement begins to spread.

1988
Mae Jemison becomes the first black female astronaut in NASA history.

1947 1954 1960s 1988 1993 2017

1954
The Supreme Court rules that segregation of public schools is unconstitutional.

2017
The Women and Minorities in STEM Booster Act, which would help make STEM fields more accessible to African American women, reaches the House of Representatives.

1993
Joycelyn Elders is appointed by President Bill Clinton as surgeon general of the Public Health Service.

INTRODUCTION

FROM INEQUALITY TO OPPORTUNITY

Across countless cultures and time periods, inequality has existed. Fortunately, many recognize the inequalities that continue to exist and make great efforts to erase them. Throughout history, there have been many attempts to correct injustices done to groups of people. The American Revolution saw the birth of a country filled with citizens who dreamed of a self-governing future. Those who fought the British for independence wanted more freedoms for themselves and future generations. Then, almost 100 years later, another war was waged that acknowledged that freedom had not been given to every American citizen. The American Civil War was a very important and long overdue attempt to correct the tragic wrong of slavery, committed against generations of African Americans.

Although more than 150 years have passed since the Civil War ended and slavery was abolished, the inequality that initially existed has never completely disappeared. Prejudices and racism still exist.

In addition, women have consistently struggled throughout American history to gain positions of power and respect that are given to men automatically. Women had to fight for their right to vote in the 20th century, much like black men did in the 19th century. Considering these two groups have faced significant hurdles in their attempts to gain equal rights, black women would seem to face the biggest struggle of all.

African American women have always needed to work extra hard to achieve greatness—especially when pursuing goals that are traditionally pursued by white men. Historically, black women have been extremely underrepresented in many industries. This is particularly true of STEM careers. STEM is an acronym that stands for science, technology, engineering, and math. In the 21st century, it is not unusual to see black women as scientists, astronauts, engineers, and doctors. As recently as 50 years ago, however, it was almost unheard of. Women traditionally either stayed home to raise children without pursuing a career at all, or they became teachers, secretaries, or career assistants. Black women often had to find domestic work, such as cooking and cleaning for other families.

Hidden Figures

The fact that the world can now see African American women as presidents of companies, brain surgeons, and astrophysicists may be taken for granted, but many individual women had to work hard to become the first black women in their fields. These women often had to overcome racism and sexism to prove their abilities and to succeed in their chosen careers. In 2016, a nonfiction book and its accompanying film, *Hidden Figures*, focused on three such women who worked for the National Aeronautics and Space Administration (NASA) in the 1960s. These women—Katherine Johnson, Mary Jackson, and Dorothy Vaughn—worked for NASA as human "computers." They were hired to solve math problems that were required for space launches. All three women were aware of their intelligence and capabilities, and through hard work, they each achieved far superior positions within NASA—but not without a lot of resistance from the white men in power.

Hidden Figures was met with a great deal of praise and achieved success as both a book and a film. This is not just because they were well-made works, but also because people love a success story, especially one about beating the odds. Many black women in the past decades and centuries have lived similar stories to Johnson, Jackson, and Vaughn in all sorts of careers and fields—movie studios just have not made movies about them yet.

Role Models

In 1981, Paula Quick Hall of the American Association for the Advancement of Science reported from a survey:

Increased use of minority and women scientists as role models in the media was urged by some who expressed the need for motivating, encouraging and providing suitable models for minority students at every level ... Young women may view a career as a [scientist or a] mathematician

The film Hidden Figures *was very popular, both critically and financially.*

as a desirable and an attainable goal if they can identify in some way with a person [from the same race and background] who has attained a similar goal.[1]

Hall demonstrated the most important reason that a film like *Hidden Figures* is necessary: It illustrates to young African American girls that they can be just as successful as anyone from any race and that they can grow up to choose any career they wish.

Nurturing parents or guardians will tell their daughters that they can be anything they want to be when they grow up. However, once those girls get a bit older, they may realize that most of the people in their chosen STEM fields do not look like them. This can make young women feel as if pursuing a career in science or medicine is not appropriate or too difficult, and they may decide against it.

Stereotype Threat

Some girls are not discouraged from choosing careers in STEM fields, but once in these careers, they are still subject to stereotype threat. This means that women may fear they may confirm a stereotype. For example, if they do not perform as well as men on tests, they are proving that negative assumptions about how women perform are

Scientific careers should be presented as possiblities for all races and genders.

true—meaning that they are less capable or intelligent. When women feel this way, stressed and anxious because they feel they must represent their entire gender, they often score lower on tests. Studies have shown that when the stereotype threat is low, women score well on difficult math tests. The stereotype threat can discourage women who start to pursue STEM careers from pursuing them further.

In recent years, colleges have noticed how gender stereotypes discourage girls from pursuing degrees in STEM fields, and they have started to make efforts to show that not all scientists and doctors are men. More and more historical biographies have been published about women in science. The toy company that makes LEGOs even started including female scientist figures to show children from a young age that these careers are not limited to men. New research, however, shows that white girls who believe negative stereotypes concerning women in STEM careers react differently than African American girls. A study conducted at Tulane University found that white girls were more likely than black girls to associate STEM professions with men. This means that black girls were not as likely to think STEM fields belonged to men. Likewise, black boys were less likely than white boys to assume that

STEM fields were more masculine.

Stephanie Rowley, from the University of Michigan, explained this difference between how white and black girls think about their futures: "What's happening with black girls is that their parents are seeing them as strong and efficacious and capable, so [they're] pushing them into whatever it is they want to do and find interesting."[2] Rowley also wrote that teachers and parents see black girls as smart and less likely to get in trouble than black boys. This gives black girls the confidence they need to pursue STEM careers from an early age. It may also make them stronger in resisting stereotypes they encounter later in life.

It is important for black girls to pursue any STEM career they are interested in because they are so underrepresented in those fields. Books and movies, such as *Hidden Figures*, help because it is good for young women of color to know that what they wish to achieve is possible. Nothing should feel out of a young black girl's reach just because of her gender or the color of her skin.

Some of the most powerful and successful African American women in history worked in STEM fields. Many of these extremely talented scientists made history by being the first black women in their career, and some of them made history by making an important medical discovery or finding a new species of marine life. It is important to recognize each of these women for their achievements—not just because they are smart and capable, but also because they beat the odds that were stacked against them from birth.

CHAPTER ONE
SPACE AND AVIATION

The story of Katherine Johnson, Mary Jackson, and Dorothy Vaughn resonated so strongly with readers and viewers because many people had no idea how instrumental black women were in the early days of NASA in the 1960s. It is surprising to many that these women were not just intelligent, they also were given the opportunity to prove this intelligence. Johnson, Jackson, and Vaughn were not the only African American women to make important advancements in the fields of air and space travel, however. There have been many black women who made waves in the fields of aviation and aeronautics.

The First Black Female Aviator

Elizabeth Bessie Coleman was both the first African American woman and woman of Native American descent to become a licensed pilot in America. Bessie was born on January 26, 1892, in Atlanta, Texas, as the 10th of 13 children. When Bessie was two years old, her family moved to Waxahachie, Texas. Her parents were sharecroppers until her father abandoned the family in 1901, forcing her mother to take positions as a cook and a housekeeper.

Bessie began attending a one-room school in Waxahachie when she was 6 years old. She had to walk miles every day to go to school, but she loved it and proved to be very good at math and reading. She completed eight grades at this school and was then accepted into Missionary Baptist Church on a scholarship for high school. She worked hard to save up enough money so that, in 1910, she could enroll herself in the Oklahoma Colored Agricultural and Normal University in Langston, Oklahoma. Her funds ran out after

Bessie Coleman is celebrated as an important figure in black history.

one semester, however, and she had to return home.

In 1915, Coleman decided to move to Chicago, Illinois, where her brothers lived. There, she worked as a manicurist at the White Sox Barber Shop. At work, she heard many stories from pilots who had returned home from World War I, and this fascinated her. Her brothers teased her about how she would never actually fly, and this made her determined to become a pilot. She got a second job to make more money, but American flight schools would not allow women or African Americans to study, so she began taking French lessons and left for Paris in November 1919 to attend aviation school.

In Paris, she learned how to fly a Nieuport 82 biplane and, in June 1921, became the first African American and Native American woman to earn a pilot's license and the first to earn an international aviation license. She later said about this accomplishment: "The air is the only place free from prejudices ... I thought it my duty to risk my life to learn aviation and to encourage flying among men and women of our [black] Race who are so far behind the White race in this modern study."[3]

When Coleman got back to New York, she received a lot of attention from newspapers, but to become successful and to support herself financially as a pilot, she would need to learn to become a stunt flier. When she discovered that she would not be able to find anyone to teach her in the United States, she returned to France and then went to the Netherlands and Germany. She came back to America and entered her first air show in September 1922 at Curtiss Field in New York under the name "Queen Bess." In this air show, which was honoring the veterans of an all-black infantry of World War I, she flew a Curtiss JN-4 biplane, which was a plane left over from the war.

The show was followed by more just like it in Tennessee, Illinois, and Texas. Her performances included many daredevil stunts, such as figure eights, loops, and dips very close to the ground and the large crowds. She quickly became known as a talented and brave pilot. Always wanting to achieve more, she traveled to California to buy her own plane. However, it stalled and crashed shortly after, and she broke her leg. Not discouraged, she lined up a series of aviation lectures in Texas. These lectures were popular and took her to Florida and Georgia, where she was featured in black theaters.

Coleman continued to see success. She was even offered an acting role in a movie titled *Shadow and Sunshine*, but refused to participate when she discovered she was supposed to portray a negative image of African Americans. Instead of becoming a famous actress, she opened a beauty shop in Orlando, Florida, and she continued to borrow planes to perform stunts at air shows. She refused, however, to perform at any air show that was still racially segregated.

On April 30, 1926, in Jacksonville, Florida, Coleman was finally able to fly her recently purchased Curtiss JN-4. Her mechanic had flown the plane from Dallas and had made three landings on the way because the plane had not been properly maintained. Although Coleman's friends and family asked her not to fly it, she was persistent. With her mechanic flying, Coleman was not wearing her seatbelt because she was planning a parachute jump the next day and needed to examine the terrain below. Shortly after takeoff, the plane malfunctioned, and the mechanic lost control, the plane diving and spinning wildly. Coleman was thrown out of the plane at 2,000 feet (609.6 m) in the air and died. Her mechanic also died when

Bessie died being thrown from a Curtiss JN-4 plane, similar to the one shown here.

the plane hit the ground and exploded. Coleman was just 34 years old.

Although Coleman died very young, she made an impact on the aviation community and the entire country. Thousands of people attended her memorial service in Orlando and 15,000 people paid their respects back in Chicago. After her death, William J. Powell—a black pilot who was famous for his civil rights activism—established the Bessie Coleman Aero Club in Los Angeles, California, in 1929, a flying school established specifically for African Americans. In 1931, the Challenger Air Pilots Association of Chicago began an annual flyover at Chicago's Lincoln Cemetery to honor Coleman. In 1977, women in Chicago established the Bessie Coleman Aviators Club. In 1995, the U.S. Postal Service issued a Bessie Coleman stamp commemorating "her singular accomplishment in becoming the world's first African American pilot, and by definition, an American legend."[4]

Rocket Scientist and Software Developer

Annie Easley was an early black female rocket scientist—even before Katherine Johnson, Mary Jackson, and Dorothy Vaughn—who developed software for *Centaur*, NASA's high-energy rocket launchers. She also contributed energy research to power plants and batteries, which enabled the eventual creation of hybrid cars, which use both gas and electric power.

Easley was born on April 23, 1933, in Birmingham, Alabama. Her parents told her that she could be anything she wanted when she grew up but that it might be hard work. Her parents emphasized a good education, and Annie ended up graduating as the valedictorian of her high school class. She then went to college at Xavier University in New Orleans, Louisiana, where she studied pharmacy for two years. She then moved to Cleveland, Ohio, and she intended to finish college. However, there was no pharmacy program nearby.

In 1955, Easley read in a local newspaper that the National Advisory Committee for Aeronautics (NACA) was hiring people to do complex mathematical equations, so she applied and within two weeks, she was hired. She was one of four black employees (out of thousands), and she analyzed math problems and did calculations by hand. NACA then became NASA and began sending objects into space. While working for NASA, she continued her education, and in 1977, she earned a bachelor's degree in mathematics from

Annie Easley was a mathematician who developed computer software for rocket launchers.

The Centaur *rocket program could not have succeeded without Annie Easley.*

VOTING RIGHTS

Before the 1960s, many unfair laws required African Americans to pass literacy tests or pay a poll tax if they wanted to vote. Easley recalled that when she submitted her application to take a test, they told her she only had to pay $2 instead of taking the test since she had gone to Xavier University. This was not the case for most African Americans because many had not attended college. Annie Easley helped other black citizens who wanted to vote study and pass the test. Unconstitutional voting tests and taxes were not eliminated until the Voting Rights Act of 1965.

Cleveland State University.

In 1958, NASA developed a booster rocket called the *Centaur*, which used a mixture of liquid hydrogen and oxygen for power. Easley's 34-year career with NASA was spent developing computer codes that analyzed alternative power technologies, which included the *Centaur*, as well as wind and solar energy projects. This is all the same technology that would be used to determine alternative energy sources for cars. Once mechanical computers started to replace humans to solve math problems, Easley adapted. She became a computer programmer, using computer languages to support NASA's programs. Her work with *Centaur* has been used to launch space shuttles, to launch satellites used for communication, to forecast weather, and for defense surveillance.

It was also used to launch the *Cassini* spacecraft in 1997 on its voyage to Saturn.

Easley retired from NASA in 1989. In a 2001 interview about being a pioneer for black women and the effects of discrimination, she said, "I just have my own attitude. I'm out here to get the job done, and I knew I had the ability to do it, and that's where my focus was ... If I can't work with you, I will work around you. I was not about to be [so] discouraged that I'd walk away. That may be a solution for some people, but it's not mine."[5] Annie Easley died in 2011.

The First Black Woman Trained as a Scientist Astronaut

In 1976, NASA trained its first black female scientist astronaut; her name was Patricia Cowings. She was a psychologist who developed training exercises for astronauts that would minimize space motion sickness.

Cowings was born on December 15, 1948, in the Bronx, a borough of New York City. Her father owned a grocery store, and her mother later became an assistant preschool teacher—after she earned her college degree at the age of 65. Cowings's three brothers would grow up to be an army general, a jazz musician, and a freelance journalist. Cowings remembers that her parents encouraged their children to make something of themselves: "Both my parents were seriously into academics as a way of getting out of the Bronx. When going to my father's grocery store I would have to do my homework in the telephone booth so he could see me working on it."[6] She remembers her father telling her, "You're not just a short round brown girl from the Bronx. What you are is a human being, and a human being is the best animal on the whole planet. Humans can achieve anything through learning."[7]

When Cowings was nine, she said, she looked around and noticed "all the good jobs were for men, and mainly for white men."[8] She always had an interest in science fiction, and science seemed like a fun game to her. Although she was not immediately good in math, she learned it as a tool. She saw scientists as "eternal students [who] ask questions for a living."[9] Her parents actively encouraged her to pursue this love of science for a living—she said they wanted her "to do what [she] wanted to do, not what someone else thought [she] should do."[10]

She went to college and graduated from Stony Brook University with honors and a degree in psychology in 1970. She then continued her education, getting both a master's and a doctoral degree from the University of California, Davis. In 1971, while she was a graduate student, Cowings started working in NASA's Summer Student Program while also investigating at Rockefeller University under Neal E. Miller, a well-known scientist in the biofeedback field. Biofeedback is what would help Cowings to later discover how astronauts could avoid motion sickness in space. She finished her doctoral degree in 1973 and then began a post-doctoral scholarship at the Ames Research Center.

In 1976, Cowings was selected as a payload specialist for Spacelab Mission Development (SMD-3). She became the first black woman in history to be trained as a scientist astronaut. That same year, she won

Patricia Cowings was NASA's first black female scientist astronaut.

BIOFEEDBACK

Biofeedback is a technique used to control bodily functions, such as heart rate. A person is hooked up to electrical sensors that receive information about the body. The feedback that the sensors pick up helps a person focus on making subtle changes in their body, such as relaxing muscles to reduce pain. Biofeedback gives a person the power to use their thoughts to control parts of the body that react reflexively, such as heart rate, sweat glands, breathing patterns, and body temperature. In 2017, many biofeedback devices are marketed for use by private citizens and can be monitored using cell phone applications.

the Space Medicine Branch of the Aerospace Medical Association's award for her investigative writings. Her paper explored how to learn to control involuntary responses to fight motion sickness in space. One of her fellow investigators on this issue was William B. Toscano, who later became her husband.

In 1977, Cowings became a research psychologist and principal investigator for Ames, where she continued to focus on physical impairments associated with working in a zero gravity environment, as astronauts did. Cowings was asked to develop a drug-free way to prevent motion sickness in space. She developed a training system called autogenic feedback training exercise, which she described as "a way in which people learn how to control up to 20 of their bodily responses so that they can keep themselves from getting sick due to motion."[11] Using autogenic therapy, a person would self-hypnotize to control their heart muscles, blood vessels, stomach, and glandular responses. Cowings claimed, "In my lab when we say 'don't sweat' we mean just that. We can teach you how to increase or decrease sweat—on command!"[12]

Multiple space shuttle missions used Cowings's work, including Space Transportation System (STS) 51-B and STS 51-C in 1985 and STS-47 Spacelab-J in 1992, which was a joint mission with the National Space Development Agency of Japan. Her experiments and research also focused on helping medical patients learn to control fainting and pilots to control nausea. She continues all this work today as the principal investigator of psychophysiological research laboratories at Ames.

The First Black Female Pilot for a Major U.S. Airline

Jill Brown was the first black woman to be chosen by the United States for training as a military pilot and was then the first to serve as a pilot for a major United States airline when Texas International Airlines hired her at age 28.

Brown was born in Baltimore, Maryland, in 1950 as the only child of Gilbert and Elaine Brown. Her father owned a construction company, and her mother was an art teacher in the Baltimore public schools. The Browns owned two homes, one near the city as well as a farm in West Virginia, where they spent many weekends and summers. Even though she was a girl, Brown was always expected to help with the chores on the farm. Her father showed her how to operate a tractor and do many things that would have been commonly considered men's work at the time.

When she was 15 years old, Brown sold vegetables that she had grown on the farm to earn money. At age 16, she worked as a painting contractor for her father's company, painting the insides and outsides of houses. When she was 17 years old, the small Brown family developed an interest in the possibilities of air travel. Jill described it: "Daddy was tired of getting speeding tickets, and one day, while they were driving past a small airport, they saw a plane landing. Daddy decided that was for us."[13] Gilbert Brown then bought his family their own plane: a single engine Piper Cherokee 180D named *Little Golden Hawk*. Jill immediately started learning how to fly it. She remembered: "Every weekend became a potential holiday. I'd take my friends flying to dinner dates, or we'd fly to our farm in West Virginia. We started calling ourselves BUA—Brown's United Airline."[14]

When it came time for college, Brown went to the University of Maryland and majored in home economics: "While my father was teaching me that I could do traditional men's work, my mother was stressing femininity ... My mother is a teacher and thinks it's the ideal profession for a woman ... I was always kind of handy in the kitchen, so I chose home economics."[15] After she graduated, she got a job teaching in Massachusetts, but she was not completely happy. It was then that she decided she wanted to become a commercial airline pilot, putting all her free time and money toward this

Texas International Airlines hired Jill Brown when she was 28 years old. The airline merged with Continental Airlines in 1982.

goal. In 1969, when she was 19 years old, she inquired with a United States military recruiter about when they would start enlisting women—the recruiters laughed at her. In 1974, only five years later, she was permitted to sign up for flight training in the U.S. Navy.

Brown was the first black woman admitted into the U.S. Navy's flight training program. Many news outlets featured her for this groundbreaking admission. Despite this attention, or maybe because of it, she only ended up staying with the U.S. Navy for about six months: "My every move was watched ... And I made some mistakes, some really bad ones."[16] Brown received an honorable discharge and left the U.S. Navy, but she was personally disappointed in the failure. Once she got home, she was so depressed that she could hardly manage to leave the house.

Eventually, Brown recovered and resumed her flight training. She went back to teaching to pay the bills, and this time, taught in Baltimore. During this period, she learned of Warren H. Wheeler, a black man who owned a small airline in Raleigh, North Carolina. She flew down to interview for the chance to work for him. Wheeler admitted that Brown was qualified to fly, but he insisted that he had no open positions for her. Brown

This is a small, private plane. This kind of plane was how Brown learned to fly.

was not going to be discouraged, and insisted: "I'll fly for nothing ... Find me a ground job just to make enough to live on, and I'll fly right now—with or without pay."[17]

Brown took a position as a ticket seller for a small salary, but she often flew in her spare time and was eventually chosen to be a co-pilot: "I was up every morning and at the airport before six A.M. for preflight ... I had to check the oil and hook up battery carts. Then I took reservations and wrote up the tickets. After that, I loaded the passengers' baggage—by myself."[18] She would then get the passengers onto the plane, climb into the cockpit, and fly. Jill logged 800 hours of flight for Wheeler, and when combined with the 400 hours she earned in Baltimore, she qualified to be a pilot for a major airline. Texas International Airlines (TIA) hired her as a pilot in 1978.

Once she had arrived at TIA, she suspected that she had only been hired for her skin color and gender. A suspicious number of special ceremonies took place when she received her wings, and she believed that the airline was using her as a way to boost its image. She left TIA after only six months to work for Zantop International Airlines, a cargo carrier in Michigan. At Zantop, she was responsible for flying materials used by the auto industry. She was on call 24 hours a day except for 1 weekend a month, and her work schedule frequently changed. Despite this stressful calendar, Brown was with them until the mid-1980s.

Brown repeatedly applied for employment with United Airlines. After being rejected three times, she filed a lawsuit against them in 1990. The case, however, was decided in favor of the airline. Brown appealed the decision, but once again, the airline won in 1997. Fortunately, Brown did not admit total defeat, and she dedicated her life to advocating for other ambitious African American aviators.

The First Black Woman to Go into Space

Similarly to Patricia Cowings, Mae C. Jemison made huge advancements for African American women in STEM careers by becoming NASA's first black female astronaut in 1988—making her the first black woman to travel into space. She also helped shape future generations of astronauts by organizing international science camps and starting the Jemison Foundation, which promotes science literacy and education.

Mae C. Jemison was born on October 17, 1956, in Decatur, Alabama,

Mae Jemison became NASA's first black female astronaut when she was 32.

but soon after, her parents moved to Chicago, Illinois, where she spent her childhood. Her mother was an English and math teacher, and her father was a maintenance supervisor. As a child, Jemison's ambitions were sky-high, but she was well aware of the obstacles she would have to overcome. The 1960s were a difficult time in America, and this was doubly true for African American girls.

Nonetheless, Jemison loved science projects all throughout grade school and would go to the public library for hours to read science books; this is where her love of stars developed. She was intrigued by the vast number of stars, how different places in the world saw different constellations, and how the same stars from history were the ones she saw.

When she was in seventh grade, Jemison's family moved from a black neighborhood to a white one in Chicago, where they were the first black family on the block. In her new school, Esmond Elementary, even though the principal doubted a black girl could achieve such high test scores, she was advanced a year to eighth grade. She remembered this experience as feeling severely out of place—the white girls at the school had probably never spent so much time with a black girl from the city.

Mae's mother encouraged and celebrated her family's heritage. Her family taught her to celebrate her race and use the word "black" as a point of pride instead of an insult. Mae was aware—even as a child—that as a black person she had to constantly prove herself to everyone, far more than a white person would have to do. Everywhere she looked, there were racial tensions in the United States; she lived through the race riots of the 1960s and Martin Luther King Jr.'s assassination in 1968. Jemison remembered being afraid of the National Guard when the Democratic National Convention came to Chicago in 1968. She had heard reports of black teenagers being shot and killed during race riots, and she knew that her race, even given her young age, would make her an easy target for angry, armed whites. She had to remind herself that she was a full citizen of the United States, equal to any of the guardsmen, and that she was not only willing to contribute to the country's future, but she also saw it as her right and responsibility.

Jemison graduated from Morgan Park High School in Chicago in 1973 and then earned two bachelor degrees from Stanford University in 1977, one in chemical engineering and one in African and Afro-American studies. She struggled in college at times,

A LOVE OF SCIENCE FICTION

Mae C. Jemison fell in love with reading science fiction books as a child. She saw science fiction as an opportunity for humans to become inspired to advance and do better. She began reading Madeline L'Engle in sixth grade, and the female scientists and heroines in *A Wrinkle in Time* made a big impression on her. In most literature of the time, women played only supporting roles; they were rarely heroes, and their actions almost never helped save the day. Fighting against this, Jemison wanted to change the real world—and she did.

balancing her identity and academic expectations. She turned to African American studies because she knew the students and professors in that program would welcome her. The same was not true in the science and engineering departments, where she was considered a second-class student and citizen. Despite having hurdles to jump over, she continued her education after graduating from Stanford—this time in medicine, earning a doctorate in medicine from Cornell University in New York in 1981.

While in medical school, she spent the summer between her second and third year in Kenya, Africa, where she volunteered with the African Medical Education and Research Foundation to provide health services to those who would not normally receive them. This experience set a foundation for her post-college life. After completing her education, Jemison traveled to Sierra Leone and Liberia in West Africa to live as a medical officer for the Peace Corps from January 1983 to June 1985. As the medical officer, Jemison had many important responsibilities, including providing crucial medical care, managing the pharmacy and lab, overseeing all medical administrative issues, and supervising the staff. Additionally, she developed an educational curriculum and taught volunteer personal health training. She wrote manuals for self-care and implemented guidelines for public health and safety so that the people of Sierra Leone and Liberia would be better equipped to offer medical care to their own people. While in West Africa, she also worked with the Centers for Disease Control and Prevention (CDC) and the National Institutes of Health (NIH) on vaccine research for hepatitis B,

schistosomiasis (a widespread para-
sitic disease in Africa), and rabies.

Making History

In June 1987, Jemison was home in
the United States and selected as one
of fifteen astronaut candidates out
of thousands of applicants. When
she completed her training in 1988,
she became the first black female
astronaut in NASA history and the
fifth black astronaut overall. Once
she became an astronaut, she was
involved in launch support activities at the Kennedy Space Center in
Florida, as well as verification of shuttle computer software for NASA.

Overall, Jemison logged nearly
200 hours in space. She was the science mission specialist on STS-47
Spacelab-J in September 1992—
the same mission in which Patricia
Cowings's anti–motion sickness
efforts were implemented. This coop-
erative mission between the United
States and Japan lasted 8 days and
orbited the Earth 127 times. Jemison
also conducted scientific experiments while in space, observing that
frog eggs fertilized in micro-gravity
developed into tadpoles normally, just like on Earth. She also

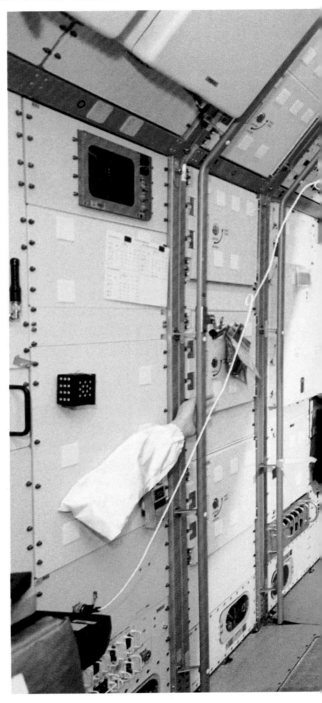

Mae Jemison spent 190 hours in space,
serving as an inspiration for other
talented African American women.

STAR TREK

In 1993, Jemison starred in an episode of *Star Trek: The Next Generation*. She was the only crew member who had actually been into space. Jemison played Lieutenant Palmer in the sixth season episode titled "Second Chances." She was very enthusiastic to be a part of this television program because Star Trek consistently showed that humans of all genders and ethnicities belonged in space. She was the first real astronaut to appear on the show, but she was not the last. E. Michael Fincke and Terry Virts later made guest appearances on *Star Trek: Enterprise*.

investigated the loss of calcium in astronauts' bones during flight—which was a major health concern—on other NASA missions.

Jemison left NASA in 1993 with a feeling of accomplishment. She explained that her role in spaceflight gave her a visible platform from which she could discuss how important it is for humans—regardless of race—to treat each other and this planet responsibly. After leaving NASA, she established the Jemison Group, which worked on projects such as the use of satellite telecommunication to more efficiently bring health care to developing countries, such as those she had helped while serving in the Peace Corps.

CHAPTER TWO
BIOLOGY AND CHEMISTRY

The first letter of STEM stands for the sciences, and the field of science can encompass many different careers, discoveries, experiments, and adventures. In much of modern pop culture, scientists are depicted as white men in lab coats doing all the important research and getting all the praise and glory. This is entirely untrue. Many brilliant black women have made invaluable contributions to the fields of science over the past century, and it is important that everyone knows who they are.

A PhD in Chemistry

Marie Daly was the first African American woman to get a doctoral degree in chemistry. Her research on the links between cholesterol and clogged arteries was vital to understanding heart attacks. She conducted important studies on how cholesterol affects the heart, how sugars affect arteries, and how proteins are produced in the cell. She also developed programs to increase enrollment of minority students in medical schools.

Daly was born in Queens, New York, on April 16, 1921. Her father was an immigrant from the British West Indies and worked as a postal clerk. He had a strong interest in science and had intended to become a chemist, but ran out of money trying to complete his education. This love of science, however, was successfully passed on to his daughter.

Daly graduated from the all-girls Hunter College High School, which was taught by an all-female faculty. There, she was encouraged to pursue chemistry and then enrolled at Queens College, from which she graduated in 1942 with her bachelor's degree. She then completed her master's degree in chemistry in just one year at New York University (NYU) while working as a part-time lab

assistant at Queens College. After graduating from NYU, Daly continued tutoring chemistry students and entered the chemistry doctoral program at Columbia University. By that time, World War II was at its height, which enabled women to pursue careers in fields that had previously been dominated by men. Under Mary L. Caldwell, an expert on digestive enzymes as well as the first female chemistry professor at Columbia, Daly studied how compounds produced in the body participate in digestion. Daly's dissertation was titled "A Study of the Products Formed by the Action of Pancreatic Amylase on Corn Starch," and she graduated in 1947, making her the first black woman to earn her PhD in chemistry in the United States.

After graduating, Daly briefly taught at Howard University. In 1948, she received a grant from the American Cancer Society to research the composition and metabolism of components of the cell nucleus. She worked with A.E. Mirsky at the Rockefeller Institute of Medicine in New York for seven years, studying proteins constructed within the cells of the body. While at the Rockefeller Institute, Daly learned from fellow scientists, such as Lenor Michaels and Francis Peyton Rous, about revolutionary studies on DNA. In 1955, she returned to Columbia

Marie Daly was the first black woman to earn a PhD in chemistry in the United States. She graduated from Columbia University (shown here) in 1947.

University to teach biochemistry at the College of Physicians and Surgeons.

While at Columbia University, she worked with Quentin B. Deming, who was famous for his research on how chemicals influenced the heart's mechanics. Together, they studied the underlying causes of heart attacks and discovered that cholesterol was part of the problem. In 1960, Daly began teaching at the Albert Einstein College of Medicine and remained there until she retired in 1986. There, she continued to study the effects of cigarette smoke on lungs and the relationship between high cholesterol and clogged arteries with Deming.

Daly served as a member of the Board of Governors of the New York Academy of Sciences from 1974 to 1976 and became a fellow of the American Association for the Advancement of Science. After retiring, Daly established a scholarship fund in 1988 for black science students at Queens College in honor of her father. In 1999, she was selected by the National Technical Association as one of the top 50 Women in Science, Engineering, and Technology. She died in 2003 at the age of 82.

Biology, Zoology

Margaret S. Collins was an African American zoologist who discovered a new species of termite and contributed valuable research to termite studies. She was born in Institute, West Virginia, on September 4, 1922, as the fourth of five children. Collins later said that Institute was "unusual in that it was an all Black town *and* a college town; in fact, the college *was* the town. As a result, there were a lot of educated Black people living there."[19] Her father had a master's degree and taught vocational agriculture at West Virginia State. He ran the school's poultry program and served as the county agent for the U.S. Department of Agriculture. Her mother never completed a college education, but she loved to read and encouraged this in her children. Collins remembered: "My parents collected an impressive library for their income level, and a regular feature of the evenings would be one member reading aloud to the rest of the family—with the youngest on the lap of the reader, in my case. I learned to read by following the finger of the reader."[20]

She grew up not only reading, but also playing in the woods and the barn around her home. This unique childhood is how she developed a curious and scientific mind. She became very interested in the world around her and was eager to learn more:

I suspect that plenty of books

Margaret S. Collins eventually taught at Florida A&M University.

and early, unrestricted reading were quite important. Hearing about scientists doing adventurous things [was] probably important. Perhaps the biggest influence of all was contact with individuals who found the discipline of biology fulfilling—enthusiasm sometimes behaves like an infectious agent.[21]

In 1936, Collins received a college scholarship to West Virginia State. She intended to major in biology, but she lost interest during her first year and consequently lost her scholarship, so she worked summers as a maid to continue paying for school. Even in school, she continued to explore nearby rivers and streams, looking for new critters. One day, while wading in the Kanawha

Margaret Collins dedicated her life's research to termites, shown here.

River, she collected samples of an unfamiliar marine animal and brought them back to Toye George Davis, a black biologist with a Harvard education—but he could not identify the animals either. Those samples were sent out to be identified and while waiting for them, Collins rediscovered her love of biology by looking through microscopes with Davis. Davis then gave her a job as a lab assistant for a small salary.

Collins completed her biology degree in 1943, with minors in physics and German. She then went to the University of Chicago to earn her doctoral degree in zoology in 1949, emerging as one of the first black women to do so. At the University of Chicago, her thesis advisor was Alfred E. Emerson, a legendary termite expert, who had the largest termite collection anywhere in the world. They sparked a friendship and a shared interest that would last for decades. Her thesis was titled "Differences in Toleration of Drying Among Species of Termite," and it is often cited in studies that were published after.

In 1951, Margaret married Herbert L. Collins and got a job teaching at Florida A&M University. In 1953, she began self-funded field studies that became the focus of her career. With her family, she would collect specimens in Everglades National Park and

Highlands State Park to study Florida termites. At this time, Collins was becoming better known in the biology field. When she was invited to speak at a nearby predominately white university, however, the school received a bomb threat as a result, and the invitation was taken away. This marked a time when Collins began to become more involved in civil rights issues. In 1956, when there was a boycott of a bus company in Tallahassee, Florida, due to segregation, she volunteered to help drive African Americans to and from work. Her involvement in civil rights activities took away from her dedication to science, however. She did not have the time to publish as often as she once did, but she still pressed on: "A lot of people opposed our civil rights efforts. I had to do what I thought was the most important thing. That's all there was to it."[22]

In 1961, Collins received a National Science Foundation grant for one year of study at the University of Minnesota, and she also studied at the Minnesota Agricultural Experimental Station, where she researched North American termites. In 1963, she became a professor at Howard University in the zoology department. She continued to study termites, later claiming, "My work has helped to clarify an issue related to the evolution of glue-squirting termites. The other concept of evolution held that there were two separate evolutionary branches of termites. We proved that this was not the case."[23]

In 1968, with financial support from the Smithsonian Museum and Howard University, Collins traveled to Mexico to research. In 1969, she became a professor at Federal City College, which is now the University of the District of Columbia. In 1972, she traveled to Arizona with support from the United States IBP Desert Project and the National Science Foundation. During this time, she also became a visiting professor at the University of Arizona at Tucson. In 1977, she traveled to Georgetown, Guyana, to test the country's potential as a scientific host nation to a conservation society. The next year, she received official Guyanese government sponsorship. In Guyana in 1979, she began researching defense mechanisms in termites and the chemicals that termites use to defend themselves from predators. She made regular trips to Guyana from 1980 to 1984.

Collins retired from Howard University in 1983, and then she became an unpaid research associate at the Smithsonian Institution's National Museum of Natural History, updating and preserving the termite collection. The Women's Committee, a group at the Smithsonian, funded most of this research. In 1992, the Smithsonian's Biological Diversity Program opened the Center for the Study of Biological Diversity in Guyana, and in 1994, 72-year-old Collins returned to Guyana to collect specimens she needed to determine a new termite species. Her five decades of work included the evolution of termites, various termite species' tolerance of high temperatures, defensive behavior in South American termites, termite ecology, and behavioral ecology. She died in April 1996 as one of the world's oldest active field scientists.

Jewel Plummer Cobb

Jewel Plummer Cobb spent her career pushing for greater inclusion of minorities and women in STEM careers. She also discovered which compounds were the most damaging to cancer cells, researched ways to alter cell growth, and experimented with growing human tumor tissue outside of the human body. She was the first black female president of the California State University, Fullerton, and was one of the first black women to head a major university in the western United States when appointed in 1981.

She was born Jewel Isadora Plummer in Chicago on January 17, 1924, and was an only child. Her grandfather had been born into slavery but became a pharmacist once he was freed. Her father was a doctor, and her mother was a gym teacher. Jewel said that science and the accomplishments of African Americans were regular topics at her family's dinner table. She later remembered, "I was raised to think that no career was out of bounds. It was always understood that my friends and I would go to college."[24]

After high school, she attended college, making it to the University of Michigan. However, because black students were not allowed to live on the university's campus, she soon transferred to Talladega College in Alabama, which is a historically black college. There, she earned a bachelor's degree in biology in 1944. She then received a fellowship to New York University, where she earned her master's degree and then a doctorate in cell biology in 1950.

After school, Cobb joined a research team at the Cancer Research Foundation of Harlem Hospital in New York where she studied chemotherapy. She worked toward determining the best dosages of anticancer medications to give to patients and used time-lapse photography to record the effects the medications had on the cancer cells. Her research focused specifically on skin cancer and the ability of melanin to protect skin from damage. She spent years documenting how hormones, ultraviolet light, and chemotherapy medications could cause changes in cell division. She published 36 journal articles related to her research. She also became affiliated with the Marine Biological Laboratory in Woods Hole, Massachusetts. She returned there repeatedly throughout her career to conduct research as an independent investigator.

In 1952, Cobb returned to Chicago to teach, and she headed the tissue culture lab at the University of Illinois. In 1960, she moved to New York to teach biology and cell physiology at Sarah Lawrence College, and then in 1969, she moved to Connecticut for seven years as a professor of zoology and Dean of Arts and Sciences at Connecticut College. In 1976, she became the dean of Douglass College, which was the women's college at Rutgers University. In 1981, she was appointed as the first black woman to be president of California State University, Fullerton. Before Fullerton hired her, however, she was denied the same position at Hunter College in New York, and her rejection led to many accusations of racism and sexism at the school.

With Cobb as their president, Fullerton saw a lot of growth. She

Talladega College (shown here) was where Jewel Plummer Cobb earned her bachelor's degree.

oversaw the construction of three new buildings and the university's first on-campus housing development. She was very concerned about the lack of women and minorities in fields of science and technology, and she worked hard throughout her career to improve the college's diversity. She told Diane Ross, then-president of the Association for Women in Science, "I think I'd like to be remembered as a black woman scientist who cared very much about what happens to young folks, particularly women going into science."[25] She received almost two dozen honorary degrees and many awards during her career, including the Lifetime Achievement Award for Contributions to the Advancement of Women and Underrepresented Minorities in 1993 from the National Science Foundation. She died in January 2017 when she was 92.

Marine Biology and Earthly Geology

Joan Owens was one of the first African American women to contribute to the field of marine biology. She redefined how button corals are classified, and she discovered several new species of corals.

Owens was born on June 30, 1933, in Miami, Florida. Her father was a dentist, and her mother was a former teacher. Growing up so close to the ocean encouraged Owens's dreams of becoming a marine biologist. At the time, however, this career was not open to African Americans. She entered Fisk University in 1950, but the school did not have a marine biology program—and neither did any other historically black colleges.

At Fisk, Owens majored in fine arts to pursue a teaching career, since marine biology did not seem to be a likely option. After graduating in 1954, she continued at the University of Michigan. She started a master's degree program in commercial art but transferred to a psychological services program in the school of education. She graduated in 1956 and spent two years working with children with disabilities at the Children's Psychiatric Hospital in Ann Arbor, Michigan. She then taught English to college freshmen at Howard University. In 1964, she began working for the Institute for Services to Education in Newton, Massachusetts, developing programs for teaching English to high school students who had been educationally disadvantaged. These programs served as a model for the Upward Bound Program, a U.S. Department of Education initiative that prepares first-generation college students for success.

By 1970, the marine biology field had finally advanced enough to offer opportunities for black scientists. Luckily, Owens had not lost her interest, even at 37 years old. That same year, she started in George Washington University's geology program. By majoring in geology with a minor in zoology, Owens received the equivalent of a degree in marine biology. In 1976, she began teaching geology at Howard and conducting her own research. This research focused on corals.

While working on her doctoral degree, the Smithsonian Institution invited her to study a collection of corals that had been obtained during a British expedition in 1880. She then became fascinated with button corals, which got their name because of their size and shape. These corals live below the level of the ocean that gets sunlight and typically live alone, as opposed to the corals that make up reefs. Owens's first research explored the evolutionary

Though the most recognizable corals are those in reefs, Joan Owens dedicated her life to researching other types of coral.

CORALS

Corals are invertebrates that live underwater. Invertebrate means an animal that does not have a spine, such as a jellyfish or a squid. These creatures sometimes develop a hard shell, such as crabs, lobsters, and snails. Corals typically live in colonies and make up reefs, including the Great Barrier Reef in Australia. The colonies are made up of polyps, which are very small, sac-like animals with tentacles that surround a mouth. Over many years, the colony develops a large skeleton. Some corals catch small fish using the stinging cells on their tentacles, but most corals get their nutrients from the algae that live on them.

changes in the button corals' skeletons, and she reclassified all known species.

In 1986, Owens discovered a new genus—meaning a new group of related species—of button coral that she named *Rhombopsammia*, and she named a species in that genus, *Letepsammia franki*, in honor of her husband Frank, whom she married in 1973. In 1992, Owens began teaching marine biology at Howard University until her retirement in 1995. She continued to conduct research after her retirement until she died in 2011.

CHAPTER THREE
MEDICINE

A nother impactful STEM career a woman can choose to pursue is medicine. Those who have dedicated their time and energy to medicine have helped humanity improve quality of life, cure diseases, and lengthen lifespans. Among the notable thousands of medical practitioners, many African American women have made big and small advancements in medicine that have touched the lives of millions of people around the world. Though they had to overcome countless obstacles, including racial and gender discrimination, remarkable female African American doctors, researchers, and nurses have established themselves as excellent role models to young black girls who also aspire to heal.

A Medical Barrier Broken

Rebecca Lee Crumpler was the first African American woman to become a physician in the United States in 1864—one year before the end of the American Civil War. Her book, *A Book of Medical Discourses*, published in 1883, was one of the first medical books written by an African American.

Rebecca was born in Christiana, Delaware, in February 1831 as Rebecca Davis. She grew up, however, in Pennsylvania, raised by an aunt who took care of sick neighbors. In 1852, Rebecca moved to Charlestown, Massachusetts, to work as a nurse. In 1860, she applied to medical school and was accepted into the New England Female Medical College, which would later become attached to the New England Hospital for Women and Children, founded by Israel Tisdale Talbot and Samuel Gregory.

The New England Hospital for Women and Children was established in 1862 with the purpose to "furnish women with medical aid from

A BOOK

OF

MEDICAL DISCOURSES

IN TWO PARTS.

PART FIRST:
TREATING OF THE CAUSE, PREVENTION, AND CURE OF INFANTILE
BOWEL COMPLAINTS, FROM BIRTH TO THE CLOSE OF THE
TEETHING PERIOD, OR TILL AFTER THE FIFTH YEAR.

PART SECOND:
CONTAINING MISCELLANEOUS INFORMATION CONCERNING THE
LIFE AND GROWTH OF BEINGS; THE BEGINNING OF WOMAN-
HOOD; ALSO, THE CAUSE, PREVENTION, AND CURE OF
MANY OF THE MOST DISTRESSING COMPLAINTS
OF WOMEN, AND YOUTH OF BOTH SEXES.

BY

REBECCA CRUMPLER, M. D.

BOSTON:
CASHMAN, KEATING & CO., PRINTERS,
FAYETTE COURT, 603 WASHINGTON ST.
1883.

*Rebecca Lee Crumpler was the first female African American physician.
She was renowned for her medical writings.*

competent physicians of their own sex and to provide educated women with an opportunity for practical study in medicine."[26] The hospital was quickly successful because women were more comfortable with the idea of being cared for by female doctors, especially in cases where they might not have gone to a doctor at all if a man was to treat their issue. The hospital treated all kinds of patients, including black women and babies, and it did not practice segregation. They had "visitors," or women hired for short periods of time without pay to talk and read to patients, and they found that the reaction to these visitors was very positive because it gave the patients affection and emotional encouragement to help their recovery. This practice is among the earliest documented cases of hospital volunteers in America.

Despite the positive environment that the New England Hospital for Women and Children provided, almost all American doctors then were white men, and they were not afraid to communicate that they doubted this institution. Many thought that women lacked the physical strength required to practice medicine. Many also thought that women were incapable of learning a medical curriculum because the topics were too sensitive. In 1860, there were only 300 female doctors out of more than 50,000 in the United States; none of those 300 were black women. The first historically black medical school in the United States, the Howard University College of Medicine, did not open until 1868. In 1864, Crumpler became the New England Female Medical College's first and only African American graduate—the school closed in 1873—and the country's first African American female doctor.

That same year, Rebecca married Arthur Crumpler and began a medical practice in Boston, Massachusetts. However, once the Civil War ended in 1865, the Crumplers decided to move to Richmond, Virginia, which Rebecca saw as "the proper field for real missionary work, and one that would present ample opportunities to become acquainted with the diseases of women and children."[27] In Richmond, Crumpler worked under Orlando Brown, the assistant commissioner of the Freedman's Bureau for Virginia, which helped more than 4 million slaves make the transition from slavery to freedom. It was not easy working in the South, however, and Rebecca faced daily sexism and racism from fellow doctors while she tried her best to treat a large number of former slaves.

After four years, the Crumplers returned to Boston and moved to

Hyde Park, New York, in 1880. She continued to work and published *A Book of Medical Discourses* in 1883. The book's first part focused on "treating the cause, prevention, and cure of infantile bowel complaints, from birth to the close of the teething period, or after the fifth year." The second part contained "miscellaneous information concerning the life and growth of beings; the beginning of womanhood; also, the cause, prevention, and cure of many of the most distressing complaints of women, and youth of both sexes."[28] It was one of the first medical books written by an African American. She dedicated it to "mothers, nurses, and all who may desire to mitigate the afflictions of the human race."[29] Crumpler paved the way for black women to enter into the medical field by being the first to become a doctor in a year in which many African Americans were still enslaved. She illustrated great bravery by fighting sexism and racism to pursue the career of her choice.

Treating Leprosy

Alice Ball was the first African American and the first woman to graduate from the University of Hawaii with a master's degree. She went on to discover an injectable oil that was the first effective treatment for leprosy.

Ball was born in Seattle, Washington, on July 24, 1892, as the third of four children in a middle-class family. Her grandfather had been a famous 19th century photographer, and her father was a newspaper editor and a lawyer. In 1902, her family moved to Honolulu, Hawaii, but when Alice's grandfather died, they all moved back to Seattle. Alice attended high school there and did very well, particularly in science. She graduated in 1910.

For college, Ball attended the University of Washington, where she earned two bachelor's degrees: one in pharmaceutical chemistry and one in pharmacy. She then decided to return to Hawaii and earned her master's in chemistry at the College of Hawaii (now called the University of Hawaii). Upon her graduation, she was the first woman and first African American to graduate with a master's degree from the school. She decided to stay in Hawaii and teach, and she became the school's first black instructor in the chemistry department.

While teaching at the College of Hawaii, Ball was recruited by Harry T. Hollemann to research chaulmoogra oil and its potential effectiveness in treating patients with Hansen's disease—commonly known as leprosy. Chaulmoogra oil comes from seeds of the chaulmoogra tree, which grows in

Hawaii. Topical applications of the oil had helped the affected area on patients, but doctors were looking for a stronger and more effective treatment. Doctors had tried to ask patients to swallow the oil, but it tasted terrible and caused stomachaches.

Ball succeeded in making the oil from these seeds water soluble, which made it possible to inject the oil into the patients. This was something that many older, accomplished pharmacologists and chemists had not been able to do. Ball was a 23-year-old black woman among a field of white men, and hers was the only success. Tragically, soon after Ball made this discovery, she accidentally inhaled chlorine gas. She became very sick and could not publish the results of her discovery. She died in December 1916.

After Ball died, the president of the College of Hawaii, Arthur L. Dean, continued her research. He made and distributed large quantities of the injectable drug and published all the work under his own name. He never mentioned Alice Ball, and he named some of the discoveries after himself. In 1918, 78 leprosy patients were released from Kalihi Hospital in Hawaii after being treated with these injections. It took decades for Ball to be acknowledged for her work. Hollemann later admitted

Alice Ball discovered the first effective treatment for leprosy, a disease that has plagued humanity for centuries.

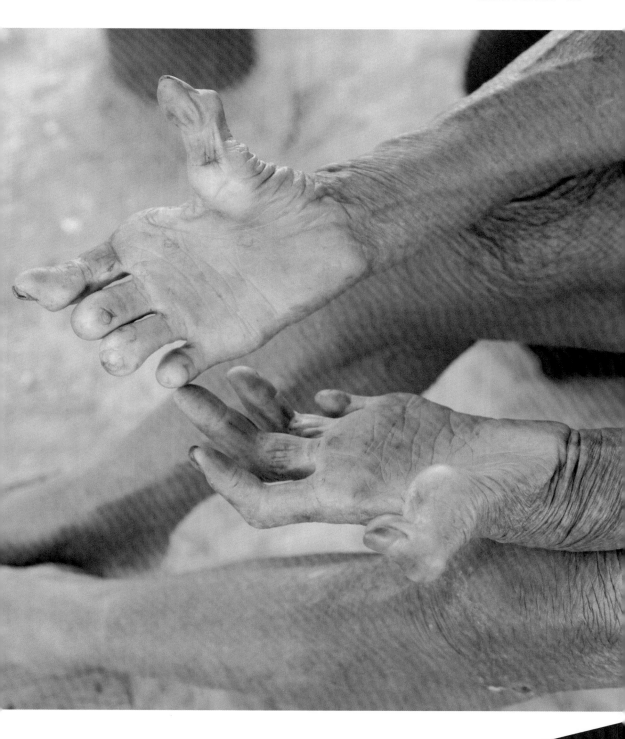

that "the neglect may have been due to both sexism and racism which may explain why both birth and death certificates list her and her parents as white ... that may have made life easier for them."[30]

In 1977, Kathryn Takara of the University of Hawaii began to research black women in Hawaii and discovered Ball's story. Thanks to Takara's work, the world can now recognize Ball's brilliance and her remarkable achievements. In 2000, the university dedicated a plaque to her on the school's chaulmoogra tree. Mazie Hirono, the lieutenant governor of Hawaii at the time, declared February 29 as Alice Ball Day, to be celebrated every four years. In March 2016, *Hawaii Magazine* included Ball in a list of the most influential women in Hawaiian history.

The oil that Alice Ball used to treat leprosy came from chaulmoogra trees, shown here.

LEPROSY

Leprosy is a long-term bacterial infection. People can be infected with the disease for five to twenty years before they show any symptoms. Symptoms include an inflammation of the nerves, skin, and eyes. The disease can sometimes lead to the lack of ability to feel pain in the inflamed area, and, in the past, doctors would sometimes have to remove body parts due to infection in unnoticed wounds. Leprosy is contagious, and in the early 20th century, people who had the disease lived in isolated communities. Most of those affected lived in poverty as social outcasts.

Surgical Success

In 1950, Helen Octavia Dickens was admitted to the American College of Surgeons, which is an education association of surgeons who pass a set of difficult qualifications. Dickens was the first black woman to be admitted to the college and was also the first black woman to become a board-certified obstetrician-gynecologist in Philadelphia, Pennsylvania.

Helen was born on February 21, 1909, in Dayton, Ohio. Her father was a former slave and had been raised by a Union colonel after gaining his freedom; he changed his name to Charles Dickens after meeting the famous British novelist of the same name. Sadly, racism and prejudice prevented him from finding anything better than janitorial work. Still, Helen's parents enrolled her in desegregated schools to make sure that she got the best education possible.

Dickens decided that she wanted to become a doctor. Luckily, she became acquainted with Elizabeth Hill, who was the first African American doctor to graduate from the University of Illinois, and Hill helped her register for medical school. Dickens graduated from the University of Illinois with her bachelor's degree in science in 1932 and her medical degree in 1934. Upon graduation, she was the only black woman in her class.

After graduating, Dickens completed an internship at Chicago's Provident Hospital, a black hospital, treating the poor for tuberculosis and working in the obstetrics department, which focuses on childbirth. After her internship, her first job was at Virginia Alexander's Aspiranto Health Home in Philadelphia

The American College of Surgeons admitted Helen Octavia Dickens in 1950. Its current Washington, D.C., location is shown here.

FIRE COMMAND
CENTER

in 1935. At Aspiranto, Dickens practiced both general medicine and gynecology for those living in poverty, often in difficult conditions. She once had to deliver a baby at night in a home that had no electricity. Dickens had to move the bed to the window and deliver the baby by streetlight. After this situation, Dickens had four hospital beds installed at Aspiranto.

After six years, Dickens returned to Provident Hospital in Chicago to continue practicing obstetrics. In 1943, she married a fellow doctor, Purvis Sinclair Henderson, and they moved to New York. She took a position at Harlem Hospital to work under surgeon Peter Marshall Murray. In 1945, Dickens earned her master's degree in science from the University of Pennsylvania Medical School, and then in 1946, she completed her residency at Harlem Hospital and became the first black woman to be certified by the American Board of Obstetrics and Gynecology.

In 1948, Dickens returned to Philadelphia as the director of Mercy Douglass Hospital's department of obstetrics and gynecology, where she stayed until 1967. Two years later, in 1950, Dickens was admitted into the American College of Surgeons, becoming the first African American female member. She also began teaching at the University of Pennsylvania. When she left Mercy Douglass Hospital in 1967, she decided to open a clinic that specialized in helping teenage mothers. The clinic offered counseling, therapy, and education to support young mothers. Dickens wanted to educate women to empower them. She led research efforts to lower the number of teen pregnancies and sexually transmitted diseases.

Her humanitarian efforts also extended to awareness of racial injustices. In 1969, she was named the associate dean in the Office of Minority Affairs at the University of Pennsylvania. Within five years of holding this position, she increased minority enrollment to the university from three to sixty-four students. Dickens received awards from the Girl Scouts of Greater Philadelphia and the American Cancer Society for her work in cancer services and education—including conducting tests to detect cervical cancer. Dickens died in 2001, and her daughter continues her legacy by practicing medicine in Philadelphia.

The Surgeon Who Developed Breakthrough Cancer Treatments

Jane C. Wright was a black, female oncologist who found less invasive ways to administer chemotherapy to cancer patients. She also developed ways to test these treatments on isolated cancer cells instead of living patients or laboratory mice. She pioneered the use of the drug methotrexate to treat breast and skin cancer. By 1967, she was the highest ranking African American woman in any American medical institution.

Jane was born in New York City on November 30, 1919, into a family of doctors. Her father, Louis T. Wright, was one of the first black graduates of Harvard Medical School and the first black doctor appointed to a staff position at a municipal hospital in New York City. In 1929, he became the city's first black police surgeon and then established a cancer research center at Harlem Hospital. Jane's grandfather and uncle were also doctors, and her younger sister Barbara would go on to become one as well.

Jane C. Wright received a good education growing up and attended Smith College in Massachusetts for art but later changed to a medical major. After graduating, she enrolled in the New York Medical College, where she received her medical degree in 1945 with honors. She then completed residencies at Bellevue Hospital from 1945 to 1946 and Harlem Hospital from 1947 to 1948, specializing in internal medicine. After her residencies, she was hired as a physician with the New York City public schools, but after six months, she left to work with her father, researching cancer at Harlem Hospital.

Louis T. Wright was researching anticancer chemicals, and Jane joined him in performing patient trials. In 1949, the two of them began testing a new chemical on leukemia, and several patients went through remission, meaning they were free of cancer. When Louis died in 1952, Jane succeeded him as head of the Cancer Research Foundation at only 33 years old. Three years later, she accepted a position as associate professor of surgical research at New York University and director of cancer chemotherapy research at New York University Medical Center.

Wright's research focused on studying how various drugs affected cancerous tumors. She was the first doctor to identify the drug methotrexate, which was very effective against tumors and then used in chemotherapy. This discovery made chemotherapy a proven treatment against cancer and helped save countless lives. She also worked hard to experiment with these drugs to increase effectiveness of chemotherapy while minimizing side effects. She developed a treatment that increased the expected lifespan of skin cancer patients by up to a decade.

In 1964, President Lyndon B. Johnson appointed Wright to the President's Commission on Heart

Jane C. Wright was the highest ranking black woman in U.S. medical institutions in 1967.

Disease, Cancer, and Stroke and the National Cancer Advisory Board. That same year, she became one of the founding members of the American Society of Clinical Oncology. In 1967, Wright was named professor of surgery, head of the cancer chemotherapy department, and associate dean at New York Medical College. This was the highest post ever held by an African American woman in medical administration. There were only a few hundred black female doctors in the United States at the time. In 1971, Wright became the first female president of the New York Cancer Society.

Wright retired in 1987, having published more than 75 research papers on the topic of chemotherapy. She led teams of oncologists to China, Russia, and several countries in Africa and Eastern Europe to study cancer treatments.

At a college reunion in 1992, she said, "I am grateful that my family supported me in all my activities, counteracting the prevailing attitudes of gender and racial discriminations."[31]

Surgeon General Joycelyn Elders

Joycelyn Elders is a pediatrician who was the first black woman to graduate from the University of Arkansas Medical School. She was a vice admiral in the Public Health Service Commissioned Corps and the first African American woman to be appointed as surgeon general of the United States, the leading spokesperson on matters of public health in the federal government.

Joycelyn was born Minnie Lee Jones in Schaal, Arkansas, on August 13, 1933, as the oldest of eight children to Haller and Curtis. The family had very little money, no electricity, and no running water, so the children had to work in the cotton fields and sometimes hunted raccoons for food. When she was 15 years old, she won a scholarship from the United Methodist Church to go to college. In 1952, she graduated from Philander Smith College in Little Rock, Arkansas, with a bachelor's degree in biology. She then changed her name to Joycelyn.

In May 1953, Elders joined the U.S. Army, where she trained as a physical therapist. After the army, she attended the University of Arkansas Medical School and graduated in 1960 as the first black woman in the medical school's history. She completed her residency in pediatrics at the University of Arkansas Medical Center. In 1967, she earned a master's degree in biochemistry. By 1976, she was a professor at the University of Arkansas Medical Center, where she focused her research on endocrinology and became an expert

Joycelyn Elders became the first black woman surgeon general of the United States in 1993.

on childhood development.

In 1987, then-Arkansas Governor Bill Clinton appointed Elders as the director of the Arkansas Department of Health, making her the first African American woman to hold the position. While in office, she improved the immunization rates for two-year-olds and achieved significant growth in the number of children who were screened for early childhood diseases. She reduced the teen pregnancy rate by making birth control and sex education more available. She also improved access to HIV testing, breast cancer screenings, and hospice care for the elderly. In 1992, she was elected president of the Association of State and Territorial Health Officers.

In September 1993, after Bill Clinton became the president of the United States, Elders was named surgeon general of the Public Health Service. She was the first African American to hold the position. She was very enthusiastic about her responsibilities, and said, "I went to Washington, not to get that job but to do that job. I wanted to do something about the problems that I saw out there that were happening in our country. I wanted to do something to make sure that all people had access to health care. I wanted to do something to reduce teenage pregnancies and begin to address the needs of our adolescents."[32] She was a controversial choice for surgeon general—she argued for universal health care coverage and was an advocate for health education, including sex education in schools. She gave speeches across the country about the importance of sex education and issues of women's health: "It makes no sense that the richest country in the world can't take better care of its women. And we all know that the health and wealth of a nation is directly related to the health and education of its women."[33] She even argued for the possibility of drug legalization. Because of these controversial opinions, she was forced to resign from her position after only 15 months, despite President Clinton's initial support.

After her brief tenure as surgeon general, Elders returned to the University of Arkansas Medical Center to work as a professor of pediatrics, where she remained until 2002. After retirement, she continued to dedicate her life to speaking across the country about the importance of health education: "If I could make any changes at all to the current health care system, you know I would start with education, education, education. You can't educate people that are not healthy. But you certainly can't keep them healthy if they're not educated."[34] Even in her 80s, Elders

AFFIRMATIVE ACTION

Affirmative action is a policy in employment or education that favors people who may have suffered from discrimination because of their race, gender, or background. Its goal is to support those who may have been disadvantaged from birth to allow equal access to education or compensation for work. Despite its successes, affirmative action has long been a controversial subject. In 2003, the U.S. Supreme Court decided that colleges could consider race when deciding who to admit to their schools. In other countries, such as the United Kingdom, this is illegal because it does not treat all races equally.

Alexa Canady publicly recognizes that she became successful, in part, because of affirmative action; she came from a disadvantaged social group and was given a chance to prove herself because of affirmative action policies.

was organizing the Changing the Face of Medicine campaign, which is a program trying to double the percentage of black doctors in America by 2030.

Advancing in Neurosurgery

Alexa Irene Canady was the first African American to become a neurosurgeon. She specialized in pediatric neurosurgery and conducted research at Wayne State University. Canady was born in Lansing, Michigan, on November 7, 1950, as the second of four children. Her father was a dentist, and her mother was the first African American elected to the Lansing Board of Education, having been very active in Lansing city affairs. Both of her parents went to college; they knew the importance of

education and instilled this in Alexa and her siblings from a young age.

However, Alexa and her younger brother were the only two black students in their school, and this posed many obstacles. Despite racial injustices, Alexa excelled in school and earned very good grades and test scores. She went to college at the University of Michigan, where she graduated with a bachelor's degree in zoology in 1971 and then her medical degree in 1975. Immediately after school, she became a surgical intern at the Yale-New Haven Hospital from 1975 to 1976 and then became the first black female neurosurgery resident in the country's history when she started her residency at the University of Minnesota.

In 1981, Canady briefly took a

position at the University of Pennsylvania and the Children's Hospital of Philadelphia, but she quickly returned to Michigan in 1982 to take a position at the Henry Ford Hospital in Detroit as a teacher and a neurosurgeon. In 1987, Canady became the director of neurosurgery at Children's Hospital of Michigan and remained there until she retired in 2001. She was nationally recognized for making the hospital's neurosurgery department one of the country's best.

Canady was inducted into the Michigan Women's Hall of Fame in 1989, and she was awarded three honorary degrees from the University of Detroit-Mercy, Roosevelt University, and University of Southern Connecticut. She publicly credits affirmative action as playing a part in helping her achieve her goals. In her retirement, she continues to mentor young African Americans in their decision to follow the profession of their choice—despite prejudices or stereotypes.

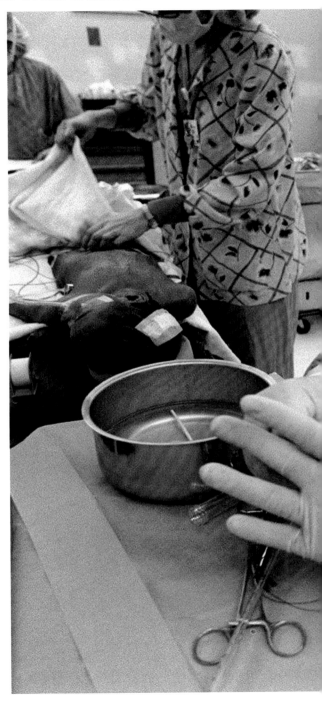

Alexa Canady, shown here, was the first black woman to become a neurosurgeon in the United States.

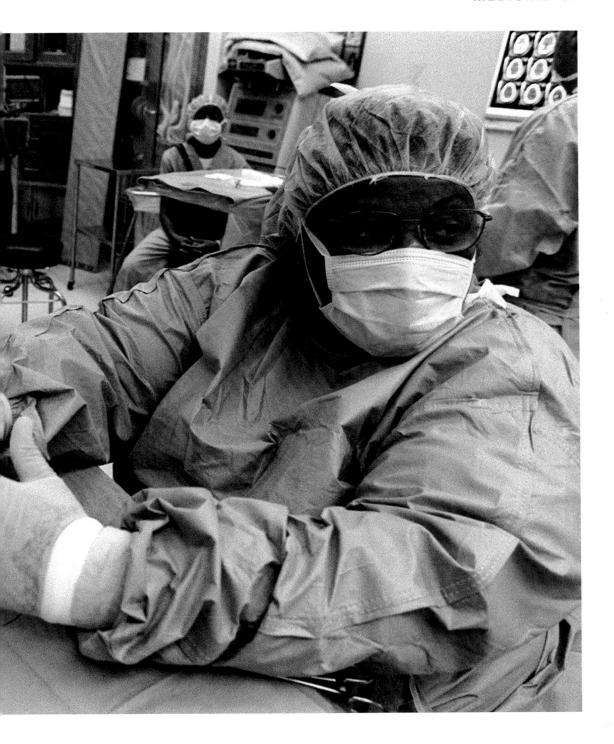

CHAPTER FOUR

PSYCHOLOGY AND PSYCHIATRY

A healthy mind is just as important as a healthy body. Just as there were advancements made in medical fields by African American women, there were also improvements made in the area of mental health. Psychology was a popular field of study at historically black colleges in the early 20th century. Students discovered that they could use what they learned in school and apply it back home in their communities to help improve them.

A Psychological First

Ruth Winifred Howard was the first African American woman to earn a PhD in psychology. She went on to become a psychologist who first published a study on triplets from a wide range of ages and ethnicities. Her career included social work, nursing, and developmental and clinical psychology. She described her work at the Abraham Lincoln Center in Chicago as "serv[ing] the needs of thickly populated communities of differing cultural and economic [means]."[35]

Ruth was born on March 25, 1900, in Washington, D.C., as the eighth child of a reverend at the Zion Baptist Church. She would later write that her father's position in the community had a lot to do with her desire to work with people as a psychologist. After high school, Ruth enrolled at Simmons College to study social work. At Simmons, she learned that many women needed support, especially those who were unemployed or undereducated and troubled youth.

Howard graduated from college in 1921 with her degree in social work and began working with the Cleveland Urban League. She then accepted a position with the Cleveland Child Welfare Agency, where she worked with children who lived in dysfunctional homes or foster care. She noted while working for these agencies that many others working in this environment of schools and child clinics "didn't understand or [sympathize] with cultural groups other than their own. This was markedly true about Negroes for whom they had firmly fixed preconceived ideas."[36]

The chief psychologist of the Cleveland Board of Education encouraged Howard to pursue a career in psychology. She was granted a Laura Spelman Rockefeller Fellowship to study at Columbia University's Teachers College and School of Social Work from 1929 to 1930. She then transferred to the University of Minnesota, where she completed her doctoral degree in psychology in 1934. Upon graduating, she registered at the Institute of Child Development, where almost all the students were women. Here, she "studied the developmental history of 229 sets of triplets, ranging in age from early infancy up to 79 years. This work, eventually published in both the *Journal of Psychology* (1946) and the *Journal of Genetic Psychology* (1947), was the most comprehensive study of triplets of its time."[37]

Howard completed an internship at the Illinois Institute of Juvenile Research and worked at a community hospital and state school for delinquent girls. She became a supervisor at the National Youth Administration and began a private practice with her husband, Albert Sidney Beckham, who was also a psychologist.

In 1944, Howard published a study of play interviews with kindergartners and fourth graders, focusing on how the way children played could indicate certain attitudes. She was involved in many organizations: she helped organize the National Association of College Women and was an active member of the American Psychological Association, the International Psychological Association, the International Council of Women Psychologists, the Women's International League for Peace and Freedom, and the Friends of the Mentally Ill. She was a longtime volunteer for the Young Women's Christian Association and Bartelme Homes, which was named for Judge Mary Bartelme, the first female judge in Chicago's juvenile court system. Howard also served as a psychologist at various institutions for most of the 1960s.

In 1983, Howard wrote an autobiographical essay in which she paid tribute to women psychologists who have contributed to the development of the field: "I salute women psychologists as they receive recognition within their field and when they help other women attain their potential."[38] She died in Washington, D.C., in February 1997.

Segregation and Self-Image

Following closely behind Howard, less than a decade later, Mamie Clark was one of the first African American women to earn her doctorate in psychology. As a social psychologist, her research on black children's self-image was instrumental in establishing the harm of segregated schools during the *Brown v. Board of Education of Topeka* case.

Clark was born in Hot Springs, Alabama, on April 18, 1917. Her father, Harold, was a well-respected doctor, and her mother, Katy, helped with his practice when black doctors were still very rare. Mamie graduated from high school in 1934 and enrolled at Howard University as a physics and math major. At Howard she met her future husband Kenneth, who was a psychology major. It was Kenneth who convinced Mamie to switch her major.

In 1938, Clark graduated college and took a job in the law office of William Houston. Houston was a major player in civil rights cases. It was at this law firm that Clark learned a lot about the psychological effects of segregation on children. In 1943, as the only black student in the program, she earned her doctorate in psychology from Columbia University. Her master's thesis was titled "Development of Consciousness of Self in Negro Preschool Children," and it was finished 15 years before the landmark *Brown v. Board of Education of Topeka* case.

After she finished her PhD, Clark briefly worked for the United States Armed Forces Institute in the 1940s as a research psychologist, but she did not enjoy it, quitting to take a position at the Riverdale Home for Children in New York, where she counseled homeless black girls. In 1946, Clark established the Northside Center for Child Development in a basement apartment in Harlem. She wanted to offer a home environment for children while providing social workers, psychiatrists, and general doctors.

In the 1940s, the Harlem public schools were telling parents that their kids were mentally ill when the children just had learning disabilities. There was also shame associated with being mentally ill at the time, so most parents would not seek out help for their children if they thought they had a problem. Clark wanted to help these kids. In her research, Clark learned that intelligence quotient (IQ) tests being given to children were racially and economically biased toward white kids: "Following psychological testing it was found that most of the children were in fact above the intelligence level placement in [special education] classes (IQ=70) and that actions on the part of public school personnel were illegal in those schools located in minority and deprived areas."[39]

Clark decided to continue the study she had started with her doctoral thesis. She focused on the self-identification of children in nursery school. She wanted to determine the racial preferences of black children when it came to choosing a doll with which to play. She gave three-year-old black children sheets of paper with drawings of an apple, a leaf, an orange, a mouse, a boy, and a girl. The kids were given 24 crayons, including brown, black, yellow, white, pink, and tan, and were asked to color the little boy or girl the same color they were and then color the picture of the opposite gender the color that they wanted to be. The results were that the black children with light skin colored the picture true to life, while the darker skinned African American kids colored the picture with the yellow or white crayons—some of them even used red or green instead of brown or black.

Clark believed that the children's choice of crayon color indicated emotional anxiety concerning the color of their own skin. They wanted to be white, or they pretended to be white. Similarly, when the black kids were presented with a white doll and a black doll and asked which they preferred to play with, more than half the children rejected the black doll and chose the white one. To be sure that the children could identify the difference between the colors of the dolls, Clark would have them first hand her the darker doll and then the lighter one.

The conclusion was that segregation in schools was causing adverse effects on African American children. They saw that white children had an advantage and given a choice, being white was the better option. This work on racial discrimination was a significant contribution in the field of developmental psychology and racial psychology, and contributed to the desegregation of schools. Clark received a Candace Award for Humanitarianism from the National Coalition of 100 Black Women in 1983 and died of cancer that same year when she was 65 years old.

Racism and Health

Jeanne Spurlock was a black female psychiatrist who was largely responsible for bringing awareness of the effects of poverty, racism, and sexism on health to the medical community. She researched the impact of racism on childhood development and ways

BROWN V. BOARD OF EDUCATION OF TOPEKA

The *Brown v. Board of Education of Topeka* case is considered one of the greatest United States Supreme Court decisions of the 20th century. It was a court case in 1954 that ruled that racial segregation of children in public schools violated the Equal Protection Clause of the 14th Amendment. This was a significant decision because it demonstrated that the U.S. Constitution could be used to argue in favor of racial equality, and it led to the end of school segregation in America.

Before this case, segregation in schools was legal, so long as the black and white schools were "equal." However, it was clear that nearly all segregated school systems abused this way of doing things.

In the early 1950s, lawyers began suing school districts to allow black children to attend the better-equipped white schools. One of those lawsuits was *Brown v. Board of Education of Topeka*. When the federal district dismissed the case, it was brought to the Supreme Court, which found that segregation in education was doing much more harm than good, and was ultimately illegal.

to approach therapy that address the needs of minority communities. She also focused on addressing the challenges faced by single mothers, children without fathers, and African Americans who experienced what she called "survivor guilt," meaning they had uncertain feelings about their own success.

Spurlock was born in Sandusky, Ohio, in 1921 as the oldest of seven children. When she broke her leg as a nine-year-old, she had a very nega-

tive experience in the hospital, which made her realize the need for more compassionate doctors. Despite this, she thought she was too poor to attend medical school, so she chose to become a teacher.

In 1940, she entered Spelman College in Atlanta, Georgia, on a scholarship. She worked full-time while attending school, but she still could not afford the tuition. She then moved to Chicago and transferred to Roosevelt University. In

Before the landmark Brown v. Board of Education *case, segregation was a way of life in most southern states.*

1943, she was accepted into Howard University's College of Medicine and graduated with her medical degree in 1947. After school, Spurlock completed a residency program in psychiatry at Chicago's Cook County Hospital in 1950 and then a fellowship at the Institute for Juvenile Research in Chicago. She then took a position at that same institute as a staff psychiatrist. She also worked at the Mental Hygiene Clinic at the Women's and Children's Hospital in Chicago and the Illinois School for the Deaf.

In 1953, Spurlock began training at the Chicago Institute for Psychoanalysis until 1962, as well as serving as the director of the children's psychosomatic unit at the Neuropsychiatric Institute. From 1960 to 1968, she was the attending psychiatrist and chief of the Child Psychiatry Clinic at Michael Reese Hospital in Chicago. During this time, Spurlock also taught as an

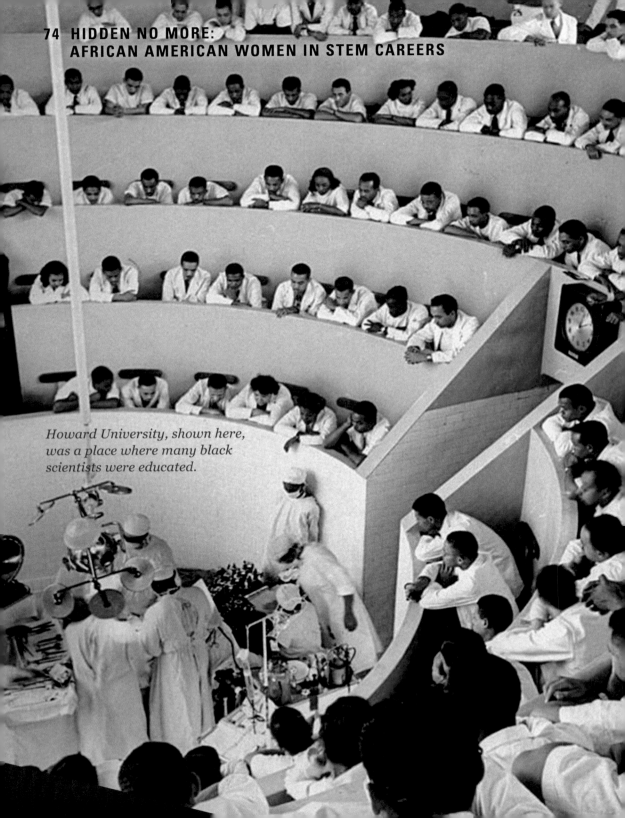

Howard University, shown here, was a place where many black scientists were educated.

assistant professor of psychiatry at the Illinois College of Medicine and maintained a private practice.

In 1968, Spurlock became a chair of the Department of Psychiatry at Meharry Medical College in Nashville, Tennessee. In 1971, she was the first African American and the first woman to receive the Edward A. Strecker Award for excellence in psychiatric care from the Institute of Pennsylvania Hospital. In 1973, she was a visiting scientist at the National Institute of Mental Health in the Division of Special Mental Health Programs in Bethesda, Maryland. In 1974, she became deputy medical director of the American Psychiatric Association, a position she held until 1991. While she was in Washington, D.C., she lobbied policymakers to ensure funding for medical and post-medical education for minorities. She was a member of the American Women's Medical Association and the Black Psychiatrists of America. She served on the Board of Directors of the Carnegie Corporation and belonged to the National Urban League, Physicians for Human Rights, and the Delta Adult Literacy Council. In 1990, she received the Guardian for Children Award from the National Black Child Development Institute.

Spurlock wrote many scholarly articles about the problems with sexism, racism, and cultural misunderstanding in the mental health field. She co-wrote a book titled *Culturally Diverse Children and Adolescents: Assessment, Diagnosis, and Treatment* in 1994 and wrote *Black Psychiatrists and American Psychiatry* in 1999, which described the experience of African American psychiatrists in academic fields, including the community of psychiatry. Spurlock died in 1999 but continues to be recognized for her work. The American Academy of Child and Adolescent Psychiatry named two fellowships after her, and the American Psychiatric Association created the Jeanne Spurlock Minority Fellowship Achievement Award and the Jeanne Spurlock Congressional Fellowship. In 2000, Spurlock was posthumously (something that occurs after death) given the Elizabeth Blackwell Award, which is the highest honor granted by the American Medical Women's Association.

CHAPTER FIVE

INVENTORS, NOTABLE WOMEN, AND THE FUTURE

Many African American women have contributed to STEM fields without specifically being a scientist, astronaut, or doctor. Many black women have invented new devices to help people who have disabilities or just to entertain the masses. Others have earned great success in fields such as architecture and helped build airports. There are always people who try to improve one aspect of life or another, and African American women have often led the charge in invention and modern approaches to problem solving.

A Talented Inventor

Bessie Blount Griffin was a physical therapist and forensic scientist who invented a way for those who had lost their arms to feed themselves independently. She also discovered new ways to detect forged documents. She was born in poverty in rural Virginia on November 24, 1914.

She attended school in a one-room schoolhouse that was used to educate former slaves and their children. She learned to read by quoting Bible verses. Bessie's family moved to New Jersey when she was in sixth grade, and she was forced to leave school. She eventually earned her GED (a high school education equivalent) and then enrolled in programs for nursing at Community Kennedy Memorial Hospital in Newark, New Jersey, which was the only black-owned hospital in the state. She also enrolled in a program for physical therapy at Union Junior College.

In 1944, Griffin went to Chicago to study physiotherapy and industrial design. She then moved to the Bronx. In the Bronx, she joined the Red Cross's Gray Ladies and worked at Veteran's Hospital Base 81, helping to rehabilitate World War II veterans who were disabled. She would tell them, "You're not crippled, only crippled in your mind,"[40] and taught them how to use their feet and teeth to hold writing utensils. This experience led her to think about new technology and techniques that might help these veterans improve their postwar lives.

At age 37, she began to work on an electronic feeding tube for people who had lost limbs. She used plastic, a file, an ice pick, a hammer, and some plates to attach a tube that was connected to a motor. Every time the patient would bite down on the tube, a bit of food would be released into their mouth. She patented her invention, and she was immediately praised for her work with the disabled. The director emeritus of the American College of Surgeons called her feeder, "a most ingenious apparatus."[41] Griffin offered to sell the United States Department of Veterans Affairs (VA) the device for $100,000, but they turned her down. She then donated her invention to the French government, which used it in military hospitals countrywide. She later claimed, "It may seem strange to be so happy over giving something that I spent five years and more than $3,000 perfecting, but I did what I thought best." She wanted to prove that "as a black female we can do

more than ... clean their toilets."[42]

Griffin also patented another device, which was essentially a bowl that could be strapped to the neck, allowing a patient to eat from it. It allowed "all persons suffering from a temporary or permanent impairment of the use of the arms and hands to conveniently and in comfort drink fluid from cups or bowls supported by the device."[43] She also came up with a way to make a disposable bile bucket out of baked newspaper, flour, and water. Her designs are still in use in some countries to this day. The woman she designed this for was the mother-in-law of Theodore Edison—the son of Thomas Edison—whose company would go on to produce some of Griffin's devices.

She also fought for the desegregation of state-supported institutions whose mission was the education of people with disabilities. She wrote columns for the *New Jersey Herald News* and the *Philadelphia Independent*. She joined activist groups to help in public relations and published several medical papers in academic journals, including one about the relationship between a person's health and their handwriting.

In 1969, Griffin started working as a forensic scientist for the police departments in several cities. She mastered how to detect forgeries and served as an influential document examiner until 1972, when Virginia centralized its document examinations. When the Federal Bureau of Investigation (FBI) rejected her because of her race, Griffin moved to England at 63 years old and became the first woman ever accepted into advanced studies at the Document Division of Scotland Yard. After this, Griffin returned to the United States and started her own forensic science consulting business, which she ran for 20 years. She examined active court cases and historical records, which included a lot of papers related to slavery and Civil War documents. When she was 93 years old, Griffin went back to her hometown to show people how far she had gotten in life: "A lot of people thought I was dead already. But I ain't gonna die now. I'm gonna live just for spite. 'Cause my work is not done."[44] Griffin died in 2009.

African American Architecture

Norma Sklarek was the first African American woman to be licensed as an architect in both New York (in 1954) and California (in 1962). She was the third black woman in the country to become an architect and helped pave the way for future black girls to pursue the career. She was the only licensed black female architect in California up until 1980.

Sklarek was born in Harlem, New York, on April 15, 1926, and was an only child. Her parents were both from different islands in the Caribbean: St. Vincent and Barbados: "Although both my parents adored me, I did lots of things with my father that ordinary girls did not do—like going fishing, painting the house, and doing carpentry work."[45] When Norma earned her first $10, she bought a book on how to draw. Norma's father worked to attain a better life for his family after he graduated from Howard University to become a doctor.

Norma's Harlem high school was almost entirely white. She got excellent grades, but her classmates mistreated her for being African American. She thought about pursuing a career in physics but decided that she preferred architecture. After high school, she took one year of classes at Barnard College in New York to prepare for the architecture program at Columbia. She continued to experience the same racism and sexism that she had in high school:

Other colleges at Columbia may have had similar gender and racial quotas, but it was quite

THE UNITED STATES DEPARTMENT OF VETERANS AFFAIRS

The VA is a federal agency that provides health care services to military veterans at specific hospitals around the country. The VA also provides disability compensation, education assistance, home loans, and burial benefits to those veterans who qualify through their three subdivisions: the Veterans Health Administration, the Veterans Benefits Administration, and the National Cemetery Administration. The agency was established in 1930, but it did not become a cabinet-level department until 1989. The primary function of the VA is to support veterans after they have served their country in the military—to show appreciation for the veterans' sacrifices and to acknowledge that transitioning back to regular life is not easy. A current problem the VA is tackling is how to prevent and end veterans' homelessness.

The United States Department of Veterans Affairs supports veterans after they come home from war—but they did not want to buy Bessie Griffin's designs in the 20th century.

obvious in architecture. The school didn't want to waste space on women. They felt that women would get married and return home to have children. The competition was fierce. I entered with a minimum requirement of one year of liberal arts, whereas many of my male classmates had bachelor's or master's degrees. Some of the students were World War II veterans receiving financial aid from the G.I. Bill. Other students had work experience as draftsmen. I was the youngest in the class, competing with mature, experienced men.[46]

Sklarek graduated from college in 1950 with only one other woman in her class. She was then turned down for a job by more than a dozen different architectural firms before she was finally hired by the city of New York. Her assignments for the city were not creative enough for her to fully utilize her talents, but she stayed for three years to get the experience required to take the test to become a registered architect. She passed the four-day exam on her first try, which was an uncommon feat. She became the first

Norma Sklarek was a key part of the construction of the Pacific Design Center, shown here.

black female licensed architect in New York in 1954.

Once she had her license, Sklarek found a position with a small firm, where she mostly designed bathrooms—but it was experience that she needed. In 1955, she was hired by one of the largest firms in the country: Skidmore, Owings & Merrill. She told her boss that she would be willing to do any project that they gave her. Her supervisor soon saw that she was very capable and intelligent and realized she was one of the most efficient employees he had. Sklarek quickly gained respect and was even asked for help by veteran architects. At Skidmore, Owings & Merrill, she never felt discriminated against because of her race or gender. She worked there for five years while she taught architecture at City College two nights a week and raised two sons.

In 1960, Sklarek moved to Los Angeles, California, and was hired by Gruen Associates, a famous firm. She got her California state license in 1962 and became California's first black female architect. After several years, Sklarek learned that Gruen had a policy against hiring African Americans, but she stayed there for 20 years and became the head of the architecture department. Her work there consisted mainly of designing shopping malls, but she also helped design the American embassy in Tokyo, Japan, and the Pacific Design Center in West Hollywood, California. While living in Los Angeles, she also taught architecture at the University of California for six years and coached students through their licensing exams.

In 1980, Sklarek left Gruen and started working for Welton Becket and Associates. Her first project was to design a terminal at the Los Angeles International Airport. The 1984 Summer Olympics were coming up, so she had strict deadlines and safety concerns. She was the only architect in her office who met her deadlines that year. After another five years, she decided to cofound her own firm—Siegel, Sklarek, and Diamond—which was the largest architectural firm owned by women in the United States at the time. She left after a few years, however, because of arguments with her partners. She then became a principal partner at Jerde Associates, which was an internationally renowned firm.

Sklarek retired in the late 1990s. She spent her retirement traveling, playing golf, and giving lectures on architecture. She died in 2012. At the time of her death, about 270 African American women were registered architects in the United States, out of 1,814 African American architects and 120,000 architects globally. She paved the way for all of those women to succeed in their careers, and she is a symbol of hope to all girls who have similar dreams.

Seeing the Future

Patricia Bath was an ophthalmologist and a laser scientist who made the removal of cataracts safer and more painless. She also cofounded the American Institute for the Prevention of Blindness (AIPB) and was the first woman chair of ophthalmology in the country when she was appointed at the University of California, Los Angeles (UCLA) in 1983.

Patricia was born on November 4, 1942, in Harlem. Her father was a motorman in the New York City subway system, and her mother—who was of African American and Native American descent—worked as a housekeeper. It was her mother who bought Patricia her first chemistry set. In high school, Patricia participated in summer internships at Yeshiva University, where she developed a math equation that accurately predicted a cancer's rate of growth when she was only 16 years old. She presented these findings at a major scientific conference in Washington,

D.C. She finished high school in only two and a half years. She later said,

Sexism, racism, and relative poverty were the obstacles which I faced as a young girl growing up in Harlem. There were no women physicians I knew of and surgery was a male-dominated profession; no high schools existed in Harlem, a predominantly black community; additionally, blacks were excluded from numerous medical schools and medical societies; and, my family did not possess the funds to send me to medical school.[47]

Bath did very well in college and earned her medical degree from the Howard University College of Medicine in Washington, D.C. Her mother kept her job as a housekeeper all that time to help her pay for school. Bath had become interested in studying medicine when she heard about Albert Schweitzer helping people suffering from leprosy in Africa. After medical school, she interned at Harlem Hospital from 1968 to 1969 and completed a fellowship in ophthalmology at Columbia University in 1970. When she completed her residency at New York University in 1973, she was the ophthalmology department's first black doctor. During this time, she also completed a fellowship in corneal transplantation. While studying at these schools and hospitals, Bath noticed something: Half the patients at Harlem Hospital were blind or visually impaired while few patients were blind at Columbia. She then conducted a study and found that blindness doubled among African Americans compared to whites.

Bath's study found that there was such an increased rate of blindness in black communities because they did not have access to ophthalmic care. She then decided to establish a new discipline known as community ophthalmology, which is now practiced worldwide. Community ophthalmology combines public health, community medicine, and clinical ophthalmology to provide primary medical care to previously ignored populations. Volunteers visited senior centers and day cares to test people's vision for cataracts and glaucoma (increased pressure in the eye that can cause loss of sight). This new effort saved thousands of people's sight because any problems they had would have gone undiagnosed and untreated. Additionally, by identifying sight problems and giving children glasses, they now had a much

better chance to do well in school. She also brought ophthalmic surgery to Harlem Hospital's Eye Clinic in 1968. She persuaded her professors at Columbia to operate at Harlem Hospital on blind patients for free while she assisted.

In 1974, Bath became an assistant professor of surgery and ophthalmology at Charles R. Drew University and UCLA. In 1975, she became the first woman faculty member in the Department of Ophthalmology at UCLA's Jules Stein Eye Institute. She did not achieve all this without facing a good amount of resistance, however. When she was at UCLA, she was offered an office in the basement, next to lab animals. She refused it: "I didn't say it was racist or sexist. I said it was inappropriate and succeeded in getting acceptable office space. I decided I was just going to do my work."[48] By 1983, she was the chair of the ophthalmology residency training program at the university.

In 1977, Bath and some colleagues founded the AIPB, with the mission to protect, preserve, and restore eyesight. Its founding principles were that eyesight is a basic human right and eye care must made available to all people, regardless of their race or how much money they have. The AIPB participated in global efforts

A person who has cataracts sees the world like the lower image shown here.

OPHTHALMOLOGY

Ophthalmology is a medical field that differs from optometry. Ophthalmology deals with the anatomy and disease of the eyeballs. An ophthalmologist performs any necessary eye surgeries, such as laser eye treatment. The first ophthalmic surgeon in Great Britain was appointed in 1727, and then in 1772, a German ophthalmologist became very skilled at removing cataracts. The first ophthalmic hospital opened in London in 1805. A female Polish ophthalmologist was the first to use lasers in her practice. The author of the Sherlock Holmes stories, Sir Arthur Conan Doyle, was a trained ophthalmologist, but the practice he opened never did well, giving him time to write.

to provide newborns with protective anti-infection eye drops, to give malnourished kids vitamin supplements, and to vaccinate children against diseases that can lead to blindness, such as measles. As the director of the AIPB, Bath traveled to perform surgeries, teach new medical techniques, and lecture at colleges.

With her research on cataracts, Bath developed a new device to remove them called the laserphaco probe in 1981. The device was ahead of its time, and she patented it. Today, it is still used worldwide. When she received the patent in 1988, she became the first female African American doctor to obtain a patent for an invention in the medical field. The laserphaco probe could recover the sight of people who had been blind because of cataracts for more than 30 years.

Bath retired from the UCLA Medical Center in 1993 and became UCLA's first female honorary medical staff member. After retirement, she remained an advocate for telemedicine, which is the use of electronic communication to provide medical services to remote areas. She never forgot where she came from or the hurdles she had to overcome to become as successful as she did.

Illusion and Invention

Valerie Thomas was an African American scientist who invented the illusion transmitter, which uses concave mirrors to project three-dimensional (3D) optical illusions. She patented it in 1980, and it has since been used in surgery, to develop television screens, and by NASA.

Thomas was born in May 1943, in Maryland. She grew up being fascinated with electronics but was discouraged by both her parents and her teachers from pursuing math and science. Despite not receiving much support for her interests, however, she graduated from Morgan State University with a degree in chemistry. Thomas was one of only two women who studied physics.

Thomas began working for NASA in 1964 as a data analyst. She developed computer data systems to support satellite operations control centers. From 1970 to 1981, she

Valerie Thomas was a data scientist for NASA, the mission control room of which is show here.

Landsat is a series of earth-observing satellites made by NASA; Valerie Thomas was a major contributor to the project.

managed the development of image processing data systems for three satellites. She became known internationally as an expert contact for Landsat data products. (Landsat is a series of Earth-observing satellites.) In 1974, she headed a team of 50 people for the Large Area Crop Inventory Experiment, which was a joint effort between NASA's Johnson Space Center, the National Oceanic and Atmosphere Administration, and the U.S. Department of Agriculture. The experiment tested the use of space technology to automate the process of predicting wheat yield worldwide. In 1985, she joined the National Space Science Data Center and was responsible for the consolidation and reconfiguration of two independent computer facilities. She served as the Space Physics Analysis Network project manager from 1986 to 1990 while it grew from 100 to 2,700 computer nodes connected worldwide.

Thomas came up with an idea for "a TV-type of application, which could transmit images and have them appear in the air in your house rather than on a screen."[49] She immediately began experimenting in her own living room with the help of her 5-year-old son, using a spoon, masking tape, a candle, and several mirrors: "Once when I was experimenting with a new mirror, I was having some difficulty finding where in space the image was being projected. And I was thinking, it doesn't seem to be working. Maybe my idea will not work! And then I heard, 'Mommy, Mommy! Here it is, right here!' So then I got excited again."[50] Her original idea was to make television 3D in the home, to bring actors right into the living room. She patented her invention in 1980 and called it the illusion transmitter. It has proven to be a remarkably versatile design.

Thomas also helped to develop computer programs that supported research on Halley's Comet, the ozone layer, and satellite technology. She received awards from NASA including the Goddard Space Flight Center Award of Merit and the NASA Equal Opportunity Medal. She has served as a role model to young black engineers and scientists. She has visited hundreds of schools and mentored many students working with the National Technical Association and Women in Science and Engineering.

Looking Forward

Though history has often been unkind to African American women, they have played an integral part in the history of science, technology, engineering, and math in the United States. Black women have made advancements in these fields that have changed the United States permanently and for the better. These women demonstrate to future generations of African American girls that their dreams can be realized—that science and technology are not fields that are strictly dominated by white men and intelligence is valued regardless of gender or race.

According to the National Science Foundation, between the years of 1973 and 2012, only 66 black women earned PhDs in physics. Between the years 2002 and 2012, the number of PhDs in computer science earned by black women doubled from 8 to 16. In 2012, black women earned a total of 684 STEM degrees. These numbers seem extremely small, however, when compared to white women, who earned a collective 6,777 degrees, while white men earned 8,478. Nola Hylton, a black female research scientist at the University of California at San Francisco, recognizes that young black girls need to be shown that there are people working in STEM fields who look like them. Otherwise, they will always believe that pursuing hard sciences is something they can never achieve.

According to the U.S. Department of Education, in 2015, African Americans held only 5.5 percent of all engineering bachelor's degrees. The National Center for Education Statistics has claimed that black women are more likely to switch their major out of STEM while in college—even though they are more likely than white women to express an interest in a STEM career, according to the American Psychological Association. These are problems that need to be addressed.

Education is the first issue—to make sure that black girls are being exposed to challenging curriculums and opportunities. One organization—ReBUILDetriot—has a goal of making Detroit, Michigan, a center for biomedical research training for racially underrepresented students. It offers a summer program to prepare students for college and tackle non-academic issues, because much of the time, they are first-generation college students and have been raised by a single parent. Many of them cannot afford books for classes. ReBUILDetroit acknowledges that one major reason for black women switching out of STEM majors is linked to pressures outside of the classroom. It aims to set up a support system for these women to prevent them from giving up. In 2016, the Michigan Science Center launched the STEMinista Project, which offers opportunities in STEM fields for girls in grades four to eight.

In addition to ReBUILDetroit, organizations such as Black Girls Code are working to encourage young women of color to develop and pursue an interest in STEM. As history shows, brilliant minds and incredible innovation are not limited by gender or race. The powerful African American women who achieved firsts in STEM fields have decisively proven—to even the strongest doubters—that everyone will suffer unless everyone has the same opportunities to invent, create, and discover. They have also paved the way for the African American women who will achieve new firsts in STEM fields in the future.

NOTES

Introduction: From Inequality to Opportunity

1. Quoted in Wini Warren, *Black Women Scientists in the United States*. Bloomington, IN: Indiana University Press, 1999, p. xiii.

2. Quoted in Alexandra Ossola, "The Different Ways Black and White Women See Stereotypes in STEM," *The Atlantic*, November 24, 2014. www.theatlantic.com/education/archive/2014/11/black-girls-stand-a-better-chance-in-stem/383094.

Chapter One: Space and Aviation

3. Quoted in "Bessie Coleman," Black History Pages, accessed August 14, 2017. www.blackhistorypages.net/pages/bcoleman.php.

4. Quoted in "Coleman, Bessie," National Aviation Hall of Fame, accessed August 14, 2017. www.nationalaviation.org/our-enshrinees/coleman-bessie.

5. Quoted in Anne K. Mills, "Annie Easley, Computer Scientist," NASA, August 4, 2017. www.nasa.gov/feature/annie-easley-computer-scientist.

6. Quoted in Betty Kaplan Gubert, Miriam Sawyer, and Caroline M. Fannin, *Distinguished African Americans in Aviation and Space Science*. Westport, CT: Oryx Press, 2002, p. 81.

7. Quoted in Gubert, Sawyer, and Fannin, *Distinguished African Americans in Aviation and Space Science*, p. 81.

8. Quoted in Gubert, Sawyer, and Fannin, *Distinguished African Americans in Aviation and Space Science*, p. 81.

9. Quoted in Gubert, Sawyer, and Fannin, *Distinguished African Americans in Aviation and Space Science*, p. 81.

10. Quoted in Gubert, Sawyer, and Fannin, *Distinguished African Americans in Aviation and Space Science*, p. 82.

11. Quoted in Gubert, Sawyer, and Fannin, *Distinguished African Americans in Aviation and Space Science*, p. 82.

12. Quoted in Gubert, Sawyer, and Fannin, *Distinguished African*

Americans in Aviation and Space Science, p. 83.

13. Quoted in Gubert, Sawyer, and Fannin, *Distinguished African Americans in Aviation and Space Science*, p. 43.

14. Quoted in Gubert, Sawyer, and Fannin, *Distinguished African Americans in Aviation and Space Science*, p. 43.

15. Quoted in Gubert, Sawyer, and Fannin, *Distinguished African Americans in Aviation and Space Science*, p. 43.

16. Quoted in Gubert, Sawyer, and Fannin, *Distinguished African Americans in Aviation and Space Science*, p. 43.

17. Quoted in Gubert, Sawyer, and Fannin, *Distinguished African Americans in Aviation and Space Science*, pp. 43–44.

18. Quoted in Gubert, Sawyer, and Fannin, *Distinguished African Americans in Aviation and Space Science*, p. 44.

21. Quoted in Warren, *Black Women Scientists in the United States*, p. 54.

22. Quoted in Warren, *Black Women Scientists in the United States*, p. 58.

23. Quoted in Warren, *Black Women Scientists in the United States*, p. 59.

24. Quoted in Daniel E. Slotnik, "Jewel Plummer Cobb, 92, Dies; Led a California Campus," *New York Times*, January 11, 2017. www.nytimes.com/2017/01/11/obituaries/jewel-plummer-cobb-92-dies-led-a-california-campus.html.

25. Quoted in Ahn Do, "Jewel Plummer Cobb, Who Broke Racial Barriers as Cal State Fullerton President, Dies at 92," *Los Angeles Times*, January 13, 2017. www.latimes.com/local/obituaries/la-me-jewel-plummer-cobb-20170113-html-story.html.

Chapter Two: Biology and Chemistry

19. Quoted in Warren, *Black Women Scientists in the United States*, p. 52.

20. Quoted in Warren, *Black Women Scientists in the United States*, p. 53.

Chapter Three: Medicine

26. Mary Roth Walsh, "Feminist Showplace," in *Women and Health in America: Historical Readings*, Judith Walzer Leavitt, ed. Madison, WI: University of Wisconsin Press, 1999, p. 513.

27. Quoted in Howard Markel, "Celebrating Rebecca Lee Crumpler, First African-American Woman Physician," PBS, March 9, 2016. www.pbs.org/newshour/updates/celebrating-rebecca-lee-crumpler-first-african-american-physician/.

28. Quoted in Markel, "Celebrating Rebecca Lee Crumpler."

29. Quoted in Markel, "Celebrating Rebecca Lee Crumpler."

30. Quoted in Jeanette Brown, *African American Women Chemists*. Oxford, UK: Oxford University Press, 2012, p. 24.

31. Quoted in Ray Spangenburg, Diane Moser, and Douglas Long, *African Americans in Science, Math, and Invention*. New York, NY: Facts on File, 2003, p. 229.

32. Quoted in "Then & Now: Joycelyn Elders," CNN, July 20, 2005. www.cnn.com/2005/US/07/18/cnn25.tan.elders.

33. Quoted in "Then & Now: Joycelyn Elders," CNN.

34. Quoted in "Then & Now: Joycelyn Elders," CNN.

Chapter Four:
Psychology and Psychiatry

35. Quoted in Ann L. Saltzman, "Ruth Winifred Howard (1900–1997)," American Psychological Association, accessed August 15, 2017. www.apadivisions.org/division-35/about/heritage/ruth-howard-biography.aspx.

36. Quoted in Saltzman, "Ruth Winifred Howard."

37. Saltzman, "Ruth Winifred Howard."

38. Quoted in Saltzman, "Ruth Winifred Howard."

39. Quoted in Robert V. Guthrie, "Mamie Phipps Clark (1917–1983)," in *Women in Psychology: A Bio-Bibliographic Sourcebook*, Agnes N. O'Connell and Nancy Felipe Russo, eds. Westport, CT: Greenwood, 1990, pp. 70–71.

Chapter Five:
Inventors, Notable Women, and the Future

40. Quoted in Sam Maggs, *Wonder Women: 25 Innovators, Inventors, and Trailblazers Who Changed History*. Philadelphia, PA: Quirk Books, 2016, p. 149.

41. Quoted in Maggs, *Wonder Women*, p. 150.

42. Quoted in Maggs, *Wonder Women*, p. 150.

43. Quoted in Maggs, *Wonder Women*, p. 150.

44. Quoted in Maggs, *Wonder Women*, p. 152.

45. Quoted in Anna M. Lewis, *Women of Steel and Stone: 22 Inspirational Architects, Engineers, and Landscape Designers*. Chicago, IL: Chicago Review Press, 2014, p. 53.

46. Quoted in Lewis, *Women of Steel*, p. 54.

47. Quoted in "Dr. Patricia E. Bath," Changing the Face of Medicine, accessed August 16, 2017. cfmedicine.nlm.nih.gov/physicians/biography_26.html.

48. Quoted in "Dr. Patricia E. Bath."

49. Quoted in Catherine Thimmesh, *Girls Think of Everything: Stories of Ingenious Inventions by Women*. New York, NY: Houghton Mifflin, 2000, p. 45.

50. Quoted in Thimmesh, *Girls Think of Everything*, p. 45.

FOR MORE INFORMATION

Books

Gubert, Betty Kaplan, Miriam Sawyer, and Caroline M. Fannin. *Distinguished African Americans in Aviation and Space Science*. Westport, CT: Oryx Press, 2002.
This book describes the lives of 20 women who excelled in aviation and space science despite poverty and prejudice.

Jemison, Mae. *Find Where the Wind Goes: Moments From My Life*. New York, NY: Scholastic Press, 2001.
This book is the autobiography of Mae Jemison, the first black woman to become an astronaut.

Lewis, Anna. *Women of Steel and Stone: 22 Inspirational Architects, Engineers, and Landscape Designers*. Chicago, IL: Chicago Review Press, 2014.
This book focuses on 22 women who have made a difference in the world as architects and engineers from the 1800s to today.

Maggs, Sam. *Wonder Women: 25 Innovators, Inventors, and Trailblazers Who Changed History*. Philadelphia, PA: Quirk Books, 2016.
This is a book that focuses on both black and white women who have achieved great things throughout history.

Spangenburg, Ray, and Kit Moser. *African Americans in Science, Math & Invention*. New York, NY: Facts on File, 2011.
This book is an encyclopedia of African American astronauts, scientists, and others who have contributed to human understanding of the universe.

Warren, Wini. *Black Women Scientists in the United States*. Bloomington, IN: Indiana University Press, 2000.
This book illustrates the struggles African American women have gone through to make scientific contributions to the United States.

Websites

African American Registry (www.aaregistry.org)
This database offers a connection to African American culture and important figures through history.

"Annie Easley, Computer Scientist" (www.nasa.gov/feature/ annie-easley-computer- scientist)
This website is NASA's biography of Annie Easley, a highly successful computer scientist.

Changing the Face of Medicine (cfmedicine.nlm.nih.gov/ exhibition)
This website contains the biographies of many women, including African Americans, who have made achievements in medicine.

Coleman, Bessie (www.nationalaviation. org/our-enshrinees/ coleman-bessie)
This is the National Aviation Hall of Fame's biography of Bessie Coleman, the first black woman to become a licensed pilot.

The Faces of Science: African Americans in the Sciences (webfiles.uci.edu/ mcbrown/display/faces. html)
This website is an index of African Americans who have contributed to science and engineering.

INDEX

PICTURE CREDITS

ABOUT THE AUTHOR

Caroline Kennon is a college librarian originally from Yonkers, New York. She got her bachelor's and master's degrees in English from St. Bonaventure University in Western New York, and her master's in Library Science from the University at Buffalo. She is an avid reader, a novice cyclist, and a cheese addict. She currently lives in South Buffalo, New York—the winters really aren't that bad.